Wings of a Dream

An Inspirational Guide to Success

Wings of a Dream
Based on a True Story

A Story of Hope

Conrad Bastien and
Joy Bastien-Brown

Copyright © 2008 by Conrad Bastien and Joy Bastien-Brown.

ISBN: Softcover   978-1-5780378-0-6

All rights reserved. No part of this book may be reproduced or transmitted in any form or by any means, electronic or mechanical, including photocopying, recording, or by any information storage and retrieval system, without permission in writing from the copyright owner.

This book was printed in the United States of America.

Contents

CHAPTER I 13
    ARTISTIC NOT AUTISTIC 15
    THE GUIDE 16
    GOING TO AMERICA 19
    IMPOSSIBLE MISSION 20

CHAPTER II 23
    FOOLISH HEARTS 28
    A NIGHT TO REMEMBER 29
    SHEEP OR WOLF 32
    HEARTACHE ON THE SHORE 33

CHAPTER III 35
    THE PRICE OF REFUGE 36
    HOMELESS, NOT HOPELESS 37
    HOPING FOR A MIRACLE 38

CHAPTER IV 41
    NEEDLE IN THE HAYSTACK 42
    A CHANGE IS GONNA COME 44
    A STORYBOOK ENDING 46

CHAPTER V 48
    IF THEY COULD SEE ME NOW 48
    ANGEL OR DEMON? 50
    ONCE IS NOT ENOUGH 52
    DANGEROUS DECEPTION 55

CHAPTER VI 57

    SHOW TIME 59
    BELIEVE IT OR NOT 61
    UNHAPPY CHRISTMAS 62
    SAVED 63
    UNBREAKABLE 65

CHAPTER VII 66

    ISLAND IN THE SUN 67
    IN RETROSPECT 68

CHAPTER VIII 73

    HERE WE GO AGAIN 74
    HIS TRUE COLORS 76

CHAPTER IX 78

    WELCOME TO JAMAICA 79
    NIGHTMARE CITY 80
    SAVIOR OR SLICKSTER 82
    WHICH WAY IS UP 85

CHAPTER X 88

    TOO GOOD TO BE TRUE 90
    THE GREAT ESCAPE 91

CHAPTER XI 94

    ANGELS IN DISGUISE 95
    LIVING A DREAM 96

CHAPTER XII 99

    MY FIRST SON 101
    SNAKEBITE 101
    NEW YORK AT LAST 104

THE SIX PRINCIPLES OF THE GUIDE 105

DESIRE 106

    MY BOSS DIANA ROSS 107
    A PRIVATE CONCERT 108
    THE OBSTACLE COURSE 109

BLUEPRINT FOR SUCCESS 109

FAITH 110

    WINGS OF A DREAM 111
    WINNING A SCHOLARSHIP 113
    COURAGE UNDER FIRE 114
    FACING YOUR FEARS 114
    THE ACTING BUG 115
    TO HER WITH LOVE 116
    "TO HER WITH LOVE" 116

WILLPOWER 117

    SALESMAN OF THE YEAR 118
    TWENTY-FIVE YEARS OF HOPING 119
    TOMORROW NEVER CAME 120
    "THE OTHER WAY AROUND" 121
    CHANGE IS INEVITABLE, GROWTH IS OPTIONAL 123

DISCIPLINE 123

    CHOICES, NOT EXCUSES 124
    SELF-ANALYSIS 125

PERSEVERANCE 126

    EDUCATION 128
    NEVER-ENDING HONEYMOON 130
    LITTLE THINGS MEAN A LOT 130

PRIDE AND DIGNITY 133

    A WOMAN CAN MAKE OR BREAK HER MAN 134
    THE MIND GOVERNS THE BODY 134
    THE MAKING OF A GENIUS 134
    IMAGINATION 136
    USE IT OR LOSE IT 137
    TO YOU, I OPEN THE GATES OF HOPE 137

This Book Is Dedicated To:

Mrs. Anna Lee Strasberg

Diana Ross

And to my mother, Sevreana "Doads" Bastien

The women who inspired this book

The women who gave me wings

As incredible as my journey to America was, there are a myriad of foreigners who have even more incredible stories. And part of their sad story is about loved ones who were not as fortunate, and lost their lives attempting to get to America.

This book will open your eyes and show that wealth, health and happiness are not just for members of an exclusive club, but for all who are determined and are ready to better their lives.

I wrote this book to show that anyone who has a burning desire, and are "truly ready" to understand and persistently apply the indispensable principles of success, can become successful.

Conrad Bastien

ACKNOWLEDGEMENTS

Special thanks to my daughter, Joy Bastien Brown, for staying up many nights to help me work on my book and for inspiring me to write the song Wings of a Dream.

Special thanks to Scott Marsigli [A North Carolina Wesleyan College Advisor] for opening my eyes, lighting my path and instilling in me the importance of telling my story.

To my dear friend, Dorothy Rose, a wonderful young lady who has always been there for me.

To my good friend, Wanda Allen, who overcame great adversity and now displays the true meaning of the word courage every day of her life.

To my dear friend, Lois Howard; thanks for your patience, understanding, and for believing in me.

To James Barnes, thank you for reinforcing my belief that yes, I can fly.

To my children, Kenny LaMothe, Conrad McRae Bastien, Lazenevou Jean Bastien, Joy Bastien Brown, Conrad Bastien Jr., Vidal Bastien, Duval Jones Bastien, Timothy Bastien, Christopher Bastien and Chianna Quick Bastien; thank you.

To my sisters, Hilda Bastien and Cecilia (Olive) Bastien, and to my brothers, Lawrence Bastien and Cecil (Joe) Bastien, I say thank you.

To all my grandchildren, a great big thank you for your support.

CHAPTER I

Adversity has always played a major role in my life. I grew up on a tiny Caribbean island passionately driven by a hunger, a burning desire to get to America and become a successful singer/songwriter.

At age nine, I was diagnosed with a learning deficiency. From that day, my single mom was like a rock. She became determined and dedicated to teaching me; I was *Artistic,* not *Autistic.*

Grief-stricken after the untimely death of my mother at age sixteen, I took my entire life savings of $35.50 and began to attempt what many saw as a mission that was impossible. With a map of the Caribbean, a daring plan and bulldog determination to get to the U.S.—or die trying—I stowed away from Trinidad aboard a ship and brazenly set out to hitch-hike through twenty-nine different islands. Defying the odds, I began making my way to the Promised Land on the wings of a dream.

My burning desire to get to America—one way or another—helped me overcome more obstacles than Indiana Jones in *The Temple of Doom.* Back then, some called it insanity; it turned out to be the greatest adventure of my life.

Let's rewind. Come with me as I go back in time. My mom left my dad when I was three months old. She took my two brothers, two sisters and I and moved in with her two divorced sisters, who lived on the other side of the island. My dad knew where we lived, but he never once took the time to visit us. My brothers, sisters and I had a very strict upbringing with our single mom and aunts. We were brought up in the church and learned to pray before we could walk and talk. Our house was like a monastery. My mom prayed aloud constantly, repeating the numerous Psalms she knew by heart many times a day, seven days a week. I couldn't help but grow up knowing these Psalms like the back of my hand because I heard them even in my sleep.

My Aunt Chrissie and Aunty Lucy also prayed a lot, but not aloud or as often as my mom. Aunty Lucy was seldom home because she worked on a sleep-in job as a maid in the suburbs and had only one weekend off a month.

My Aunty Chrissie, who took care of the housework, didn't have much to worry about because her son Lawrence Osborne was a flight lieutenant in the British Air Force in England and sent her a monthly allowance.

We were poor and lived off the land. We had no machine, but with tools in her hands, my mom would cut down the trees, till the land and plant all the fruits and vegetables we needed on our two-acre farm. We also raised a few chickens and ducks.

I didn't think so at the time, but the living was anything but easy. We lived in the hills out in the country and had no indoor plumbing, electricity, running water, or transportation. When it didn't rain, we walked with our buckets to the river two miles away, filled them with water, placed them on our heads and tried not to fall as we navigated the hills and valleys on our trip back home.

My siblings and I walked ten miles to and from school each day. For as long as I can remember, with the exception of track and field, school was not a happy time for me because I had trouble learning. For some unknown reason, I just didn't comprehend things quickly so I constantly interrupted the class asking the teacher to repeat herself. Eventually the teachers grew frustrated and the other students became aggravated and made so much fun of me that I finally stopped interrupting the class and just sat there day after day falling behind, withdrawing and wishing I didn't have to attend school.

However, the sun came out when it came time for track and field because I could run like a deer. I came alive then because no one in my class or any of the other classes could beat me in the hundred-or two hundred-yard dash. Nor could they beat me in the quarter mile or half mile race.

As always, once we were back in class, I continued to struggle with all of my subjects except reading. My mom had no idea of my learning problem in school because I threw away the notes my teachers gave me to give to my parents.

As time went by, my teachers paid less attention to me and I became more of a loner. I daydreamed often and soon began writing short stories about a shy, quiet kid who became very popular after easily beating the competition in track and winning a medal for his school. I enjoyed writing these stories so I began writing different versions of them. My brothers and sisters said my stories were stupid, but my mom would keep them and re-read each one of them and applaud me. She told me I was talented and my confidence grew.

One Sunday evening as I returned from a long quiet walk in the valley, I walked into my house and to my surprise found Mrs. Cox (my math teacher) sitting there having a talk with my mom. Suddenly I felt so ashamed I wished I could just disappear. Over the next few months, with the help of the school, my mom took me to a few different doctors in an attempt to find out why I was having so much difficulty learning in school. Then the results of several tests came back and my mother and I were called in to see the doctor.

For as long as I live, I will never forget that day. While waiting in the doctor's office, my mom seemed more nervous than ever before. I wondered if she already knew something that I didn't. The doctor came in and after some small talk he said the words that changed my world forever. "Mrs. Bastien, there's no easy way of saying this, so I'll just say it. Your son has a learning disability." My mom was speechless; she sat there just clutching her rosary.

The doctor was smooth. "Mrs. Bastien, I know how you must feel, but this is not necessarily a death sentence. With a lot of love and the right schools, many children . . ."

She interrupted him, "What do you mean the right schools, doctor?"

He said, "Well, there are special schools for children who are . . ."

She stood up abruptly, "There's nothing wrong with my son that God and I can't fix. I am not sending my son to any . . ."

He put up his hand defensively. "Mrs. Bastien, I'm sure your intentions are well-meaning and born out of love. However, the truth is you don't know very much about this affliction."

That set her on fire. She grabbed me by the hand and stepped up to him. "You may be a big time doctor with all kinds of degrees, but quite obviously you don't know very much about the power of desire or the power of prayer." She tugged my hand. "Let's go!"

To this very day, I can remember seeing the astonishment on the face of the doctor, and for reasons I did not understand at the time, I felt like laughing. I felt like saying, "I could've told you so!"

Don't misunderstand I knew something was wrong with me, but deep inside I felt it was not as serious as the officials made it. I was confident that whatever it was my mom and I would be able overcome it. From that day on, my mom went on a mission to help me overcome my learning deficiency. She went over my homework with me as many times as it took me to comprehend and remember it.

ARTISTIC NOT AUTISTIC

My mother encouraged me to write more short stories and never stopped reminding me I was *Artistic*, not *Autistic*. I didn't always take it as seriously as I should have because one day, to get my full attention, my mother out of frustration grabbed me by my shoulders and shook me.

She was in tears as she said, "As long as you live, don't you ever forget you can accomplish anything you put your mind to if you have God and the guide in you. God should be first in everything you do, and the guides are the things that can help you surmount any obstacle in your path and drive you to victory. The guides are: 1) DESIRE: That's what it starts with. Nurture it until it grows into an obsession. 2) FAITH: Without it, you're lost. 3) WILL-POWER: It will give you the fire and drive you will need to succeed 4) DISCIPLINE: It'll make you strong and give you the power you'll need. 5) PERSEVERANCE: That is your password because the race isn't always for your swiftest or the brightest. 6) PRIDE AND DIGNITY: They're your guiding lights. No one can ever take them away from you, not ever". She gently tapped my temple. "It's all up there and you have the power to turn it on. Just let it shine and it will guide you." Then she gave me a big hug and suddenly we were both in tears.

Somehow the kids in my class found out about the results of my test and, to them, I was no longer just the "slow kid." They made up brand-new names for me. I took as much as I could, then I started getting into fights. My cousin Nestor was an ex-boxer and after getting a few lessons from him and ending my last two fights with knockouts, the kids found someone else to pick on.

The next two years of schooling were extremely frustrating for me. I didn't feel or look different from the other kids and couldn't understand my inability to learn as fast as them. It was so depressing that I sometimes felt inferior and tried to quit school, but my mom wouldn't let me. She worked overtime convincing me I was just as good as any of the other kids. She constantly reassured me that if I worked really hard at it, if I truly desired it and believed I could do it, determined to persevere to the very end, I could overcome not only my learning deficiency, but also every other obstacle that would eventually stand in my way.

Long before I started school, my mom read to me quite often; apparently, it paid off because reading became my favorite subject in school. Perhaps that was the only subject I was any good at. When I did cut class—and there were a few times—it wasn't to run with the boys, it was to go to the little library and lose myself in a good book.

My mom was my very best friend. Sometimes I think she was my only friend. She was trying so hard with me I didn't always agree with her methods, but I knew I just couldn't let her down, so I repeated to her what she so passionately called *The Guide*.

THE GUIDE

"DESIRE, FAITH, WILL POWER, DISCIPLINE, PERSERVERANCE, PRIDE AND DIGNITY." I listened attentively as she patiently explained the meaning of these words to me and their importance in my life. At the time, I didn't fully understand why it was so important for me to remember these words, but I wanted to please her so I began trying to memorize the words and their meanings.

My schoolwork slowly improved as my confidence grew. I fell in love with reading and became one of the best readers in my class. I still had trouble learning and retaining things, but after seeing how hard I was trying, my teachers and even some of my fellow students were a little more patient with me.

There were lonely times late at night when I would cry for the father I never knew and wondered how different my life would be with him in it. But those sad moments were short lived because the healing love of my mother would chase away the ugly demons of loneliness from my soul.

My oldest brother and sister had lost their jobs and their wills to find another job. We were having a hard time making ends meet. So against my mother's wishes, I left school when I turned eleven to help support the family. And while many other family members seemed to accept poverty as their fate, a voice inside kept telling me I was destined for so much more. I refused to see poverty as anything more than temporary. I believed that my fate was—like my pen—in my hands. I was the author, director, and producer of this script called "my life" and I was determined to create a life for myself that would be as different from that of my predecessors as Trinidad is from America.

After leaving school at age eleven, I found work as a brick mason helper that paid $5.00 a week. I worked hard and tried to save some money, but after helping out the family, there was very little left. Every time I saw a plane fly in the sky, I wondered who was on board, where they were going, and why it wasn't me.

While other kids my age would hang out and play together, I stayed to myself, going for long quiet walks in the valley where I would sit by the river and work on my story as I daydreamed about one day becoming a famous writer.

At home, repeating *The Guide* became a ritual. Every other morning before I left for work, like clockwork, my mom would ask me to say *The Guide* to her. Whenever I had trouble remembering the words and their meaning, she patiently went over each one of them with me and then she would add, "It's more than words. It's a code you must learn to live by." I would say, "Yes, mom" and make a mental note to try harder to really understand the true meaning of the words contained in *The Guide*.

Even though I no longer attended school, my mom encouraged me to do as much reading as possible. So, taking my mother's advice, I read every book I got my hands on and the more I read, the more I became fascinated by faraway places with strange sounding names, especially the United States. I asked a lot of questions of anyone who knew anything about the United States and, in time, I came to understand that the same way many islands made up the Caribbean, many different states made up America. I tried to learn everything I could about this interesting country.

As time went by, I began feeling a stirring in my soul. It was as if something out there was calling me. I had no idea what that something was, but in my heart I knew that one day I would have to answer that calling and go in search of my destiny.

On rare occasions when I could afford it, I went to the movies and was captivated by the magic on the screen. America seemed like a wonderland, the most fascinating place on Earth. More and more, I found myself dreaming about one day going to America where the streets, I heard, were paved with gold.

After weeks of putting away fifty-cents a week, I bought the family a little radio with two stations. Soon after, I fell in love with singing and songwriting. I loved country music especially because that's mostly what my mom listened to. I spent a lot of time trying to sing like some of the singers I heard. I wrote down the lyrics to my favorite songs, studied them carefully, and then wrote my own lyrics to the melodies. After doing this for a few weeks, it became more than a habit; it became my passion. I stopped writing stories and decided I was going to become a singer-songwriter.

My brothers and sisters called me a dreamer, but my mom encouraged me to go for it and constantly reminded me I could do anything if I wanted to badly enough. "If you can conceive it and truly believe it with faith, you can achieve it." She would say this over and over again to make certain I got it.

My mom was the only one who believed in me or understood my need to dream big. Each week, I would sing the new songs I had written for her as she critiqued them for me and told me I was getting better every day. As time went by, my confidence grew. Trying even harder than I did before, I sought out and teamed up with other aspiring singers/songwriters and got myself into as many talent shows as I could. I made lots of new friends and heard lots of fascinating stories from other kids whose rich friends or parents visited America. To me America sounded like the Promised Land.

With encouragement from my mother, I kept reading as many books as I could. I briefly considered going back to school to please her, but when I remembered the way those kids made fun of my learning deficiency, I decided to put it off.

By age 13, I had grown to be six-feet tall, a little taller than my mom. However, she still had me repeat *The Guide* to her at least four times a week. By now I could recite the words and their meaning without missing a beat and that made my mom very happy.

The early 1960's was a great time to be alive and in show business. It seemed like every guy I knew was either singing in a group, singing solo or trying to sing because the singers had all the chicks.

I began living for the weekend, when I would get a chance to perform at some talent show or, if I had no money, sneak into the movies and get a glimpse of how people in America lived. New York City seemed to be the most magical but dangerous place on Earth.

One night at a friend's house, I saw Diana Ross and the Supremes on television. I was so taken with her velvet voice and her style that I began writing songs I believed would be just right for her and promised myself that someday Diana Ross would sing one of my songs.

GOING TO AMERICA

When I turned fourteen, my desire to come to America and become a rich and famous singer songwriter became an obsession. New York was all I could think of. There was one little problem, and that was I knew no one in New York and I didn't have the money for a plane ticket. In fact, I had $11 to my name. But I was not about to let such trifling inconveniences stand in my way. I began getting my papers in order and got myself a map of the Caribbean and began learning about the twenty-nine islands that stood between Trinidad and America.

One day on an impulse, I told my family about my plans and everyone except my mom fell off their chairs with laughter. They were hysterical. I wasn't surprised by their behavior and didn't blame them for not taking me seriously. After all, America was a long way off and they knew I had no money, which was all they could see. What they couldn't see was the raging fire in my soul driving me on, ready to surmount every obstacle that would dare stand in my way. They couldn't see my dreams or know that I was willing to stake my life on this decision. In the meantime, I pursued my career relentlessly and learned all I could about America.

By the time I turned sixteen, my brothers and sisters had left home, and not long after that, my mom got sick and was hospitalized. Her blood pressure was out of control. I visited her in the hospital after work each day. Even there, she worried more about me than herself. Before I left, she took my hand and made me promise her I would put God first, live by *The Guide*, and follow my dreams no matter what. I did, and she was happy. But as I promised her I would do these things, I couldn't help but wonder where all this was coming from.

The next evening, I worked late and couldn't go to see her. That's the evening she passed away and, for me, it seemed like the end of the world. When Hilda, my oldest sister, came to my job and brought me the news of my mother's death, I covered my ears and ran away, refusing to believe one single word of it. I just wouldn't accept it. To say I was devastated would be the greatest of understatements. For weeks, I remained in a state of shock, each day feeling more alone than the day before.

I didn't eat or sleep much and spent most of my days alone, wandering in the woods half expecting to see her or at least to hear her voice. At night, I would cry myself to sleep as I called out her name, hoping she would answer me. My siblings and aunts tried to help but I was inconsolable. When I did fall asleep, I kept dreaming of my mom telling me to always put God first and to live by *The Guide*. I was having the same dream even when I was awake, so I began talking to God, asking for his help. As time went by, I slowly began to accept the painful reality that she was gone and I was now on my own.

I could still feel her presence and somehow knew she would always be with me. Soon, I began feeling stronger and not so alone. I gradually began to get a grip on reality again.

I came out of mourning for my mother with a renewed sense of determination and inspiration. Somehow I was going to make her proud of me. Nothing was going to stand in my way of becoming a success. I made a promise to her and, come what may, I was going to keep it.

Not long after my mother's death, I began to see how cruel, cold, and lonely this world can sometimes be. Suddenly nothing was going right for me. I had to learn fast and grow up in a hurry. I tried to get back to my singing and songwriting, but something was blocking me. Nothing felt right and I kept coming up empty.

IMPOSSIBLE MISSION

A green light began blinking in my mind, getting brighter with time. I took that as an indication it was time for me to make a move and start chasing my dreams. I was only 16, but at 6'2 and 180lbs, I could easily pass for 18 or 19. So traveling alone should not be a problem. My map of the Caribbean showed there were around twenty-nine islands between Trinidad and the U.S, Grenada being the first and Puerto Rico the last. Further research showed there were small passenger ships that traveled between Trinidad and Puerto Rico. My daring plan was to first get to Grenada, work for two to three months, save some money, then move to the next island and do the same, continuing this process through many other islands until I got to Puerto Rico. Once there, I would then take a plane to New York.

The very thought of going on this journey sent a series of shivers up and down my spine. It wasn't fear. It was excitement, and that made me wonder if my brothers and sisters were right when they said I had to be crazy to even think of island hopping to America.

The ship I would be traveling on was leaving the next evening for Grenada, the first stop on my great adventure. Early the next morning, I went into the yard and took a long last look around at everything. I took mental pictures of the place where I grew up. After slowly walking through the lovely field of carnations, my mom's favorite flowers, I went under the house and dug up a little jar with my life's savings of $35.50. Then I went inside and packed the few things I had, including my mom's old Bible. I slowly looked around the house as though seeking assurance from the unknown. Then I got on my knees and asked God to accompany and guide me on my journey. I walked five miles to the village and caught the bus that took me down to the seaport.

I was in awe as I stood on the dock looking up at the big ships. And even though no one would confuse any of these ships with luxury liners, to me they were magnificent. I got directions and found the ship scheduled to leave for Grenada in a few hours. By now, anxiety had gotten hold of me. Before buying my ticket, since I was very early, I decided to go up and check out the inside of the ship. No one stopped me, so I climbed aboard and had a good look around. After wandering the ship unchallenged for quite a while, I found a cozy little room with lots of sheets, blankets, and towels right next to a small shower. In this room was a little bed that looked so inviting, I decided to rest for a while. That's when I remembered some of the stories I had heard about people stowing away on ships to different islands. I thought to myself that if I just stayed in here until we reached Grenada, I could save some money. If I got caught, I would tell them I was very tired and fell asleep. So I put my bags down and must have been more tired than I thought, because I really fell asleep. When I did wake up and look outside, it was pitch dark and we were well out to sea.

I pinched myself and it hurt, so I knew I wasn't dreaming. That's when I began to panic. Maybe this wasn't such a good idea after all. How will I survive for the next two days, or is it three? What if I get caught? Will they put me in jail? Should I just go and turn myself in? Before I could come to a decision, the door flew open and a heavyset man in his fifties stood in the doorway.

"Hey! What are you doing in here?" he asked.

I showed him my passport and explained to him what happened, but he didn't believe a word of it. He was going to turn me in. I had to plead with him, then bribe him with $5.00 before he calmed down. He took the $5.00, told me to keep my mouth shut, and disappeared. He later returned and for another $5.00 he offered me what appeared to be a legitimate-looking return ticket to Grenada.

"You'll need this when you get to Grenada," he said.

I was puzzled. "Why?" I asked him. "Why do I need a return ticket? I'm not going back to Trinidad; I'm going to America."

He smiled and explained it to me like he was talking to an eight-year-old. "Well, son, unless you are a citizen of the country you are going to, they won't let you in with a one-way ticket. To enter the country, you must have a return ticket."

"Oh! I see. Thank you so much!" I gave him the $5.00, took the ticket and was good to go. I breathed a sigh of relief and for the first time in a long time, I felt like dancing. Trinidad was now behind me and my journey had begun. I was on my way to the Promised Land.

On the flipside of my jubilation was the fact that $25.00 was all the money I had left to my name. I had to eat lightly until we got to Grenada. Then I had no idea where I would stay, how long it would take me to find work, or how I would survive once I got to Grenada. But I was not about to start worrying now. I felt certain God would make a way for me. I went out on the deck and looked up at the stars in the sky as the cool island breeze caressed my face. And as I thanked God for getting me this far, I saw a shooting star racing across the sky. Silently, I made a wish and believed in my heart that it would come true.

The next two days at sea turned out to be much better than I dared hope for. I was on the deck sitting on a bench in the afternoon sun, thinking of my mom and singing a song with my eyes closed. As the song ended, I heard applause and opened my eyes to find four lovely girls standing there. I stood up and introduced myself. They were Shirley and her sister Stella, Ann and her twin sister Anna. They insisted I sing another song, so I did. It was a slow love song called "Unchained Melody". As I sang, Stella became the only girl there because I found myself singing directly to her. Shirley was much prettier than Stella, but there was something special about Stella and the way she looked at me I felt a connection. The song ended and I thanked them for their applause. We talked for a while, then Anna and her twin sister left, but Shirley and Stella stayed. Shirley did most of the talking; Stella was the quiet one. I told them I was 21 and they didn't believe me, but when I told them I was really 19, they bought it.

Shirley was 19 and Stella was 21. They were from some place in Grenada called Grenville. They were returning from spending two weeks with their aunt in Trinidad. We talked for a while and promised to get together later. I avoided meeting them later that evening because I was too embarrassed to let them know I had a linen closet for a room.

The next afternoon when the girls found me, they had a guy with a guitar with them. His name was Tony. He played a mean guitar and knew lots of songs. We found a cool spot and began to jam. I sang a few songs, he sang a few songs, and soon there was a small crowd. We even invited people from the crowd to come up and sing and some of them did. We all had a very good time that afternoon.

Later that evening, the ship finally docked as darkness fell in Grenada. We wished each other well and began preparing to disembark. That's when the cold shadows of uncertainty and doubt tried to stage a very unwelcome appearance. But I was on a high from the good time I had singing with Tony and the girls and was not about to let anything bring me down. So I got my bag, shook off the fear and doubt and held my head high, as I began walking off the ship in confidence.

CHAPTER II

Trying not to look out of place, I followed the crowd as we disembarked, and it seemed like every passenger was met by a friend or relative except me. It was getting late as the dock slowly emptied. As reality set in, I began to wonder what the hell had I gotten myself into. Trying to be brave, I looked from one end of the dock to the other and pretended to be disappointed that no one had come to meet me. Over in the corner I saw two shady-looking characters and felt that they were sizing me up. I was 6'2, 180 lbs and could handle myself, but I was also on their turf. I told myself, "Just don't show any sign of fear." I turned up the collar of my jacket, put my hands in my pocket, and stared them down the same way I saw John Wayne do in the movies. Suddenly, I heard a car horn behind me. Talk about a godsend! In the cab were Stella and her sister Shirley, two of the girls I had met on the ship and become friendly with during my journey at sea.

I remember telling them I was meeting a promoter in Grenada to do a few shows before going on a tour of the Caribbean. After I told them I had been stood up by my promoter, they graciously offered me shelter at their home until I found him. I thanked them profusely as I climbed into the cab. Shirley got out and insisted I sit in the middle, so I did. I could hardly believe my good fortune. These girls were a blessing in disguise.

As the cab drove through the poorly-lit villages, I looked out the window but couldn't see much in the darkness. I did smell the wonderful aroma of spices and over-ripe fruits like mangoes, papayas, bananas, guavas and plums hanging in the warm night air, letting even a blind stranger know that he was now in a beautiful tropical island.

Time and again, I apologized to the girls for almost landing in their laps each time the cab made a sharp turn as we traveled through the hills and valleys, but they just giggled and said, "That's alright!" As we pulled up to their home, I tried to pay the cab fare, but they wouldn't hear of it. Shirley smiled and said, "You can repay us after your first big performance."

They shared a lovely three-bedroom home with indoor plumbing, kitchen, living room and dining room. They showed me to the bedroom at the end of the hall and told me to make myself at home.

We took turns showering and, after changing clothes, the girls came up with a tasty dish of codfish and zabuca, which Americans call avocado. After the meal, we moved to the living room where we sat around and talked for a while. They inquired about my family. I told them I never knew my dad, my mom died a few months ago and the rest of my family and I were not very close. I learned that Shirley, the much lovelier, light-skinned one, was nineteen, a freshman in college and was first-runner up for Miss Grenada a year earlier. Stella, the quiet, shy one, was 21 and a sophomore at college with her sister. Their parents were killed when their car went over a cliff in the mountains four years ago.

The girls themselves had been in a car accident a month before and were under doctor's orders to stay at home for the next two months. After awhile, I felt closer to the girls and was moved by their generosity and trust, so I decided to come clean and tell them the truth-except about my age. When I told them I was on a mission to hitch-hike through the Caribbean from island to island all the way to America, they asked me, "Have you lost your mind?" But when I told them there was no promoter waiting for me and that I was on my own, to my big surprise they said in unison, "We knew."

I was shocked. "How did you know?"

Shirley answered, "We also know you stowed away in the linen closet." They both fell out with laughter. I was trying to enjoy the joke by laughing with them, but I was also trying to hide my embarrassment. Then Stella rescued me by coming and sitting next to me on the couch.

There was a brief moment of silence before Stella said to me, "I'm very happy you decided to tell us the truth. That shows character."

I asked her again, "How could you have known?"

Stella said, "Our cousin told us."

I became very curious. "Who is your cousin?"

Shirley answered this time, "Fenton, the fat man who caught you in the linen closet." She leaned closer to me, "This is a small country with small villages where everybody knows everybody." She lingered playfully. "We know the people you'll need to meet if you plan on doing any shows in this town." She stood up, stretched and yawned, "But that's for tomorrow. My brain is tired and I'm going to bed." She waved at us and disappeared into her room.

I looked at Stella sitting so close to me and suddenly felt like a shy thirteen-year-old out on his first date. I looked around. "This is a beautiful home you have."

She nodded, "Thank you."

"Did you and your sister grow up here?"

"My parents built it when I was one year old. Shirley was born here."

"Any brothers?"

She hesitated. "An older brother. He died in Vietnam four years ago. He was a U.S. Marine. It was his funeral my parents were coming from when they had their accident."

"I am so sorry. I shouldn't have pried."

She shook her head, "That's alright. I don't mind talking about it."

We fell silent for a while and I wondered if we had run out of things to say. We both started to speak at the same time, then stopped. I pointed to her, "You go first."

But she said, "No. You go first."

I cleared my throat and wondered why I was so nervous. "Ok, I will. I am never at a loss for words around a pretty girl, but . . ."

She interrupted, "Pretty? You must be talking about my sister! Besides, she's closer to your age."

"No, Stella, I'm not talking about Shirley, I'm talking about you. And age has nothing to do with it."

She tried another route. "Don't you remember my sister was the runner up to Miss Grenada? She was close to having a chance at becoming Miss World."

"Yes. She told me. You must be very proud of her."

"The whole family is."

I shook my head, "I can imagine, but I'm still talking about you, Stella."

She sounded defensive, "What about me?"

I knew I had to say it just right. "When I look at you, I don't just see your body, I also see the inner you. I see the real Stella, a very beautiful person. It shows in your eyes, and your eyes are the mirrors of your soul."

She was silent for a moment. Then she said very softly, "No one has ever said that to me before . . . they usually go after my sister."

I took her hand, "Perhaps no one has taken the time to really look at you before." Her eyes became misty as she turned her head and looked away from me. I welcomed the sound of silence as I watched her biting her lip, trying not to become emotional.

I gently squeezed her hand, hoping she would say something. Then a single tear very slowly rolled down her face and at that tender moment something inside me was yearning to just hold her, comfort her, and protect her. I moved a little closer and gently turned her head to face me. For a magical moment as we gazed into each other's eyes, we heard what each other's hearts were saying and there was no need for words. I took her face in my hands and slowly kissed her. It was a long, sweet, never-ending kiss that left us shivering.

She abruptly stood up and said, "I better go now. It's very late. I'll see you in the morning." She touched my face before hurrying off to her room.

I sat there thinking that I had kissed quite a few girls, but it never felt like this before. Why was this one different? I went to my room and laid on my back, my fingers laced under my head thinking of this girl who had just taught me how a kiss could really be. I wondered if she laid awake in her room thinking about me.

Then like a cold slap in the face, I suddenly remembered promising myself not to get seriously involved with any girl. My goal was to get to America. Falling in love or having a steady girlfriend was completely out of the question. I could not afford and would not allow myself to be distracted.

I made a mental note to be sure to explain this to Stella tomorrow. I owed it to her and to myself to be honest.

I thought to myself, honesty is a characteristic of pride and dignity, and they are a vital part of *The Guide* that I promised my mom I would live by.

I awoke the next day very disoriented. For a minute, I couldn't remember where I was or what day of the week it was. Then it all came back and I stepped out of bed to look for the girls. In the kitchen, I found breakfast and a note from them telling me they would soon be back from shopping. I looked at the time. It was one-thirty in the afternoon. I couldn't believe I had slept that late.

A big smile appeared on my face when I remembered the sweet dream I had of Stella. I thought about sharing it with her, but then decided to keep it to myself. I went outside and looked around. The yard was big with lots of flowers growing everywhere. The smell of spices, the colorful birds singing in the trees, the different fruit trees dropping their ripened fruits, and the sound of steel drums coming from two or three houses away gave this tropical isle an ambiance all its own.

I went back in, took a shower and washed a few things, then went out and sat on the steps. I was enjoying the view and the warm breeze when Shirley drove up alone. I stood up, "Where's Stella?"

Shirley wore a bright pretty smile and I easily saw how she almost became Miss Grenada. "She stopped at her girlfriend's to get her hair done. Now, let me ask you a question."

I nodded, "Go ahead."

Her smile got even brighter. "What have you done to my sister?"

I was caught by surprise. "What do you mean? We didn't . . . I mean, I didn't do anything to her."

She was persistent. "You must have because I've never seen her like this . . . She dragged me out of bed this morning to go with her to pick up some new clothes. And, she never, ever gets her hair done. She usually does it herself." She was looking at me as though she expected me to reveal some big secret or something. I stood there without an answer. This news was a surprise to me too.

We went inside and talked for quite a while before Stella came home in a cab. I went outside and helped her with her packages. With her hair all done up, she looked like a different person. "Wow! You look great, Stella!"

She blushed, "Thank you." After we got inside, I waited for the right moment to handle what I considered to be a very delicate subject. I definitely needed these girls to be on my side, but not at the price of deception.

They were both in the kitchen when I said, "Girls, let's have a talk." They both looked surprised.

Shirley said, "What about?" I sat facing them and then stood up. "This is not easy for me, so please bear with me." They were all ears now. "You girls have been very understanding and very good to me. I need you. I need your help if I'm going to make it. However, I made a promise to my mother before she died to live by *The Guide*, which is a set of rules . . . a code of ethics. I also promised her I would follow my dreams, and I never break my word." They were really puzzled now.

Shirley said, "So, exactly what are you trying to tell us?"

"I am trying to say . . . well, I'm attracted to Stella. I like her more than any girl I've ever known. She's special, and perhaps she feels something similar."

Shirley said, "So!"

I spoke directly to Stella, "I don't want to get hurt and I don't want to hurt you. Maybe I'm saying this more for my own benefit, but . . . well, I am just passing through. In a while I'll be gone. I am on a mission to get to America and I must follow my dream, my destiny."

They were quiet for a moment before Stella asked me, "So why are you telling me all this?"

I didn't have to hesitate. "Because you have my mind in a whirl and I'm becoming confused between what I know I should do and what my heart is saying. Maybe I'm asking for your help. I'm just being totally honest with you. I must get back on track today, right now. I must concentrate on finding a way to get into a show or two, then hopefully putting on my own show before moving to St. Vincent." I was on a roll, so I kept going. "I don't know what the future holds for us, but I believe that if we were meant to be in time, it will happen. For now, help me concentrate on show business. Please."

Then I gave each of them a great big hug. Shirley seemed to be all right with it, but Stella seemed a little disappointed. For the next few days, we were a little formal with each other. Stella mostly stayed at home while Shirley took me around to seek out the entertainers. During the ride into town the first day, neither one of us spoke much.

The second morning, halfway into the trip, Shirley turned to me and said, "That was a very courageous and noble thing you did."

I pretended not to understand. "What are you talking about?"

"That speech you made . . . "My sister knows you're right and she admires you for having the courage to say it."

I was genuinely curious. "You think so?"

She said, "I know so . . . she still likes you a lot . . . maybe even more now."

"And I like her, but I felt we were moving a little too fast. I don't want to hurt her, not ever."

She asked, "Do you have an older brother?"

I wasn't quite sure what she said. "I beg your pardon?"

She said, "Never mind." Then we fell silent again.

This girl seemed to know everyone, from the pups to the big dogs. By the third day, she had gotten me into two upcoming variety shows. One was on Friday night at the theatre in Grenville and the other on Saturday evening at a dance hall in the city. I felt very fortunate to have met these young ladies.

For the next three days, Shirley drove me back and forth to rehearsals. When we returned home at night, Stella would have a delicious dinner waiting. During dinner the evening before the Friday night show, I told them how much I appreciated all they were doing for me and promised to pay them back double. Stella and I weren't saying very much to each other, but the need and the longing that was building up between us was thick enough to cut with a dull knife.

Shirley 'the instigator' whispered to me, "I don't know why you two don't just . . ." She left it hanging and walked away.

FOOLISH HEARTS

Each time I looked at Stella, I felt like my head was being pushed under water. Then she gave me "that look" and my heart began doing push-ups. It was as though I was being pulled under by some giant tidal wave. I was trying to refrain from making a move, trying to be strong, but I had never ached like this to hold any girl before.

Friday night came and finally it was show time. The theatre was packed and I was a little nervous. I peeped out from behind the curtains and saw Stella and Shirley sitting in the second row. Finally, my name was announced. As I ran out and grabbed the microphone, my nervousness disappeared. I did three songs and got a warm reception. However, in the middle of my last song, I completely ripped my pants while doing a split and had to play it very cool for the rest of the song. I wondered if the audience had noticed.

As the song ended, I backed off the stage. The folks behind the curtain had seen my pants rip and were falling over themselves with laughter. I had to take my shirt off and tie it around my waist because my underwear was showing in the back. When Stella and Shirley found out, they too could not stop laughing.

The show did even better than anyone expected and the promoter paid the entertainers very well. The first thing I did when I got paid was give Stella and Shirley fifty-percent of what I earned. After the show, we stopped at one of their cousin's houses and celebrated. The next day, Shirley informed us that her boyfriend Tony was taking her away for the weekend. Neither Stella nor I had any comments. Shirley looked at me mischievously, whispered something to Stella and they both laughed out loud. It was probably a dirty joke.

After thanking the Almighty and retiring that night, I laid awake most of the night thinking about being here alone with Stella the following evening. The very thought of it sent something electric right through me, and that scared me. I didn't understand the feelings that kept growing inside me. Sometimes I even fantasized about staying in Grenada with her and coming home to her every day. I began to wonder if she had put some kind of voodoo hex on me. Then I remembered *The Guide* and the promise I made to my mother. I swore to myself that nothing was going to keep me in Grenada.

After Shirley left that Saturday afternoon, Stella and I didn't talk much. We kept ourselves busy right up until it was time to call a cab to take us to the show. I took Stella to the front row, then went backstage.

The show was standing room only, and I was determined to do my best to live up to the fanfare the announcer made about me being "one of Trinidad's best." My turn came and I took the stage. I saw Stella sitting in the front row and that gave me additional inspiration. My last song was "When a Man Loves a Woman." As I began singing, I took the microphone and went on down to the audience. After singing a verse to the audience, the spirit moved me, so I took Stella by the hand and led her onto the stage where I sang the rest of the song to her. As the song ended, she was in tears, so I held her close to me.

Everyone was on their feet giving us a thunderous standing ovation that almost brought me to tears. Then the cameras came out and the people were jostling for a better position to take our picture. A few of them even came up onto the stage. When the show ended, the promoter held a little celebration party in the back room. The entertainers congratulated each other; some exchanged phone numbers and promised to keep in touch. I got two offers for upcoming shows.

A NIGHT TO REMEMBER

Stella seemed uncomfortable in the crowd and kept whispering "let's go home" in my ear. After I got paid, we turned down a few offers to go to house parties and made our getaway. We didn't say much in the cab on the way home. She put her head on my shoulder and I just held her hands.

She must have left the radio on because when we entered the house, Percy Sledge was singing "When a Man Loves a Woman." I could hardly believe it.

She closed the door and reached for the switch to turn on the lights, but I quickly intercepted her hand in mid-air and drew her close to me. "May I have this dance, angel?" We began slow dancing in the dark. This felt so good, so right, it would be sinful to deny. Yes, I know I had told myself I must not, cannot fall in love, but I guess my heart had a mind of its own.

When the song ended, I was unable to let Stella go. A little moonlight filtered through the window, showing me her lovely face. I whispered to her, "Baby, you are bewitching. I don't know whether I'm coming or going." Other than the soft music in the background, the only things that disturbed the silence was the ticking of the clock on the wall and the crazy beating of our fluttering hearts. As we looked into each other's eyes, not a word was spoken, yet everything was heard. Then everything seemed to happen in slow motion, giving my mind adequate time as it began taking snapshots of my love and I. I knew I wanted to remember this magical night forever.

I gently touched Stella's eyes, nose, and mouth as if making sure she was real, and then something inside me took over. It was a magical, multi-colored explosion in slow motion. It was the roughness and the gentleness, the yearning and the passion. The passion had built to a hunger that had to be satisfied. Moment to moment, we were caught up in an ecstasy that was almost unbearable.

Hours later, as we lay there quietly, I felt really alive for the first time in my life. "Heavenly" is the only word I can think of that would do justice if I attempted to describe the remainder of that night. It wasn't just physical; it was mental and spiritual. One of the unforgettable lessons I learned that night is there is a world of difference between "doing it with a partner" and "making sweet love with the one you love."

I awoke to a quiet Sunday morning with the birds singing right outside my window, soft music on the radio, and the girl I love asleep in my arms. I smiled and asked myself, does it get any better than this?

Shirley returned that evening looking sunburned. The very first thing she asked was, "Why are you two grinning from ear to ear?" Stella covered her face and went off to the kitchen.

I asked Shirley, "What are you talking about?"

She persisted, "You both are lit up like Christmas trees."

There was a knock at the door. It was Shelton, another one in their long line of cousins. He brought in a newspaper and turned to page three with a picture of Stella and me on stage. They made a big fuss over it while I tried to be cool and act like this happened all the time.

Later that day, I gave Stella and Shirley some of the money I made the night before and informed them I wanted to produce my own show. They encouraged me to go for it. With their help and the contacts I had made, it took me ten days to line up two soloists, Desmond Frey and Lester Short, Maxwell the comedian, and two top-notch singing groups, The Crickets and The Black Birds. I had trouble landing a good band at first, then got lucky and booked everyone's favorite, The Bad Boys. The only thing that was missing was a location. For a $50.00 deposit, I rented a theatre for the occasion. Fortunately, the entertainers all agreed to wait until the night of the show to get paid.

As usual, Shirley and Stella were a big help. After rehearsal each day, they took me all over the different villages to put up posters and hand out flyers. Things were going so well for me that it was kind of scary. I was very happy. Seven nights a week, Stella was either sneaking into my room or I was sneaking into hers. I couldn't get enough of this girl. I had become addicted to her sweet loving. In the back of my mind, I knew I would soon have to pay the piper, but oh, I was enjoying the dance.

I kept telling her daily, "This is not a very good idea. I'll be leaving soon." And yet I wouldn't, I couldn't go one night without her. My mouth was saying one thing, but my body was doing another. A part of me was lost and I didn't seem to care. Stella seemed to be in the same boat. She said she was a big girl who knew what she wanted and would take her chances rather than have no chance at all.

The night came and the show turned out bigger than anyone expected. I made some money and a lot of new contacts that night. The offers began pouring in. Things were going great and I was now in a position, thanks to Stella and Shirley, to produce my own show anywhere I wanted.

I gave Stella and Shirley fifty percent of what I made. Neither one wanted to take it, but I insisted. That night, I got on my knees, gave thanks to the Almighty and asked him to give me strength to get myself back on the right track. Everything seemed to be going great, but a red light was flashing in my mind. Something wasn't right.

The next day, I went for a long walk alone in the woods. I sat on a log and did some serious thinking. I needed to get back on track, pronto! I thought about my mother and *The Guide* and began saying it aloud. When I got to willpower, I remembered the way my mom drilled its meaning into my mind. Suddenly the answer to my problems was illuminated. That red light that had been flashing in my mind had just turned to green.

Very calmly, I got up and started walking back to the house, where I was immediately greeted by Stella. "Where were you? I was getting worried."

I threw my arm around her shoulder. "I went for a walk."

She sounded concerned. "Are you alright?"

"Yeah, I'm alright." We walked back to the house in silence.

A few days after my triumphant show at the St. James Theatre, I was contacted by an up-and-coming local promoter known as Big Barry. He was six feet-four inches tall and three hundred pounds. Barry solicited my help to put on a variety show in the same theatre where I had my show.

SHEEP OR WOLF

Barry turned out to be a local guy who was just getting started in show business and needed a lot of help. He was a very smooth talker and easily convinced us that helping him would be the right thing to do. Along with some of the artists he had lined up for the show, I put up some money to help Barry out. I was thinking, how could I say no when not long ago I was exactly where he is right now?

The other artists and I had a clear understanding with Barry that we would get back our investment as soon as the show was over, in addition to getting paid for performing the show. We all felt that this was going to be a huge success, maybe even the start of a joint business venture.

The night of the show, the theatre was sold out. We had a hit. After the show, the celebrations came to a sudden halt when we discovered that Big Barry had vanished into thin air with all the money. We were flabbergasted! This wake-up call brought me back down to earth. For the past few weeks, my life was like the days of wine and roses, but this incident reintroduced me to the real world. It was a major blow to my finances and my plans, but I was not about to let it or anything hold me back. The flashing green light in my mind was becoming even brighter. So the next day I went down to the bay and bought a return ticket on the next ship leaving for St. Vincent in three days—just one week before my seventeenth birthday.

To me, it is absolutely amazing how perceptive women are. Personally, I think women are smarter than men, but that's another story.

When we got in bed that night, the first thing Stella said to me was, "You're leaving me, aren't you?" She caught me completely off guard.

"Why do you say that?"

"It's just a feeling." She hesitated. "Am I wrong?" I couldn't bring myself to answer her. "Am I wrong?"

I whispered. "No." We didn't say much to each other for the rest of the night.

The next day, I told the girls I would be leaving. They immediately went to work on me to get me to change my mind. They reminded me of how successful the show I produced was and encouraged me to produce another one. They even volunteered to put up the money to back the show. I explained to them that my mind was not into it because destiny was calling. I had to follow my dream.

That night, surprisingly, Stella did not try anymore to talk me into staying. She knew my mind was made up. As she lay in my arms without saying a word, I could feel her tears running onto my chest. Her quiet sobbing was tearing me up inside until I decided we had only a few hours left to make this a night to remember. When we finally tried to get some sleep, dawn was breaking so we stayed up, wrapped in each other's arms, and watched the sun rise over the hills together. Then we all had a quiet breakfast, of which Stella and I ate very little. I packed and we headed to the seaport in silence.

HEARTACHE ON THE SHORE

We got to the port a little early, then got as close to the ship as we could without boarding. I hugged Shirley and thanked her for everything, and then she walked a little ways off. I held Stella and didn't know what to say.

She broke the silence "When will I see you again?"

I had to be honest. "I'm not sure." She bit her lip and tried to blink away the tears.

"Will I ever hear from you?" I held both her hands in mine.

"Sweetheart, you will. I give you my word on that. If you believe nothing else, believe that."

She took my hand and put it on her stomach. "When?"

"I can't say for sure, but you will as soon as I have a steady address." I brushed away a tear from her cheek. "Honey, listen to me. No other girl will ever make me forget about you. No one has ever made me feel the way I feel about you." I touched the left side of my chest. "You're in my heart. I am taking a part of you with me and I'm leaving a part of me with you."

She gently touched my face. "You are my love. You are."

I continued, "So if a few weeks go by and you don't hear from me, always remember to have faith. Have faith in me. Don't ever give up on us."

Behind us they began making the last call to board the ship. I kissed Stella and said, "This is so long, not good bye." And for the first time I realized what agony parting can be as her sobbing got louder as she held onto me in tears.

She sobbed, "I can't take it, I can't take it!" I quickly waved Shirley over, pulled away and handed Stella to Shirley. It was the hardest thing I've ever had to do, but it was now or never. I picked up my bag, kissed my fingers and touched her lips, then turned around and climbed aboard that little ship. And as I waved to her over and over again from the deck, the pain in my heart was too much to bear and the temptation to get off was too great, so I moved as far away from the boarding ramp as I could. Then, thank God, they removed the ramp and the ship very slowly began leaving shore. Stella was now waving like her life depended on it. And even though I knew it was too late and she probably wouldn't hear me, I leaned over the rail and shouted at the top of my lungs, "I love you! I love you!"

I wondered, why didn't I tell Stella I loved her when I had the chance? I have never felt so completely helpless in my life. At that moment, if there were any possible way for me to get off that ship, I would have gotten off and ran right into her arms.

I waved to Stella until I could no longer recognize her. Then I stood there in tears, unaware and uncaring that people were still staring at me. A lady patted me on the back, handed me some tissues and said, "It's alright! It's alright!" Finally, when I could no longer see the island, I went down to my little cabin and tried to settle down.

In two days, my ship would arrive in St. Vincent. To many of the passengers, it would be just another stop on their voyage, but to me it would be a giant step on my way to fulfilling my dream.

CHAPTER III

After leaving Grenada, I spent the next two days at sea on that small ship sailing towards St. Vincent. The sea was rough because of bad weather, but that did not bother me half as much as the longing in my heart for Stella. It took a great deal of effort for me to focus on the mission at hand. In my head, a voice kept whispering to me. "You hold a return ticket to Grenada! Use it. Turn around and go back to Stella." I ignored that voice because it was the voice of fear. I knew I needed help; in fact, I needed Divine Intervention, so I began repeating this line a few times a day: "Dear God, please give me the strength and the courage to follow my dreams and the willpower to persevere to the end." I felt so much better after making that affirmation.

During my two days at sea, I sought out the passengers who lived in St. Vincent and tried to learn as much as I possibly could about the country, like where the cheapest rent was, who the top promoters and entertainers were, and where to find the big nightclubs. If those didn't work out, my back-up plan was to find a hotel and get a job as a waiter or busboy, maybe even a dishwasher.

I smiled as I remembered the first night I landed in Grenada and good fortune smiled on me. I thought to myself, wouldn't it be nice to get that lucky again? It sure would, but does lightning strike the same place twice?

It was three-thirty a.m. and in a few hours we were scheduled to arrive in St. Vincent. I should have been asleep, but sleep was elusive. Today was D-Day for me, and I was as anxious as I was ready. The early morning sun was rising and caught us a few miles offshore. On the distant horizon, I could see the faint outline of the tiny island coming into view and the palms of my hands began to sweat. I felt like a young soldier about to go into battle for the first time. I was nervous, uncertain, but unafraid. I thought to myself, this is just another island I will have to go through to accomplish my mission.

When I came through Customs, the agents were very friendly. I showed them my passport and my return ticket, told them I was here on vacation and they sent me on my way. I took the bus to town and checked into Margo's Rooming

House, which I was told was as cheap as it gets. I was trying to conserve what little money I had left. I spent the first week talking to the top promoters and entertainers. However, I must have said or done something wrong because every one of them treated me like I was carrying a rare disease.

Later, I found out their reason for avoiding me was my address. I was staying at a whorehouse in the bad part of town. Their reasoning was I had to be flat broke and desperate to stay there. I then went to other towns and talked to other entertainers and promoters about helping me to get into an upcoming show as a guest artist or to co-produce a variety show with me, but the word was out and no one would touch me. Maybe they thought I was an out-of-town pimp.

The second week in St. Vincent, I spoke to a few more show business people in the hopes of getting on somewhere. Then I shifted my focus down to the city at night, trying to get on as a nightclub singer. By the end of my second week, no job was in sight. I had very little money left. In fact, if I ate only once a day, I would have money for two more weeks' rent, meaning I could either move out or wait to be thrown out. That's when that voice of temptation began whispering in my ear again. "Your return ticket is the answer to your problem. Use it, you fool. Turn back." I pretended not to hear, hoping that voice of doom would go away.

That night after praying, I wrote Stella and told her how much I missed her and that I was doing fine, but I did not send her a return address. I was now into my third week without work, and though I kept telling myself everything was going to be alright and I would find work any day now, the booming voice of doom was becoming louder and louder. It was now week four and nothing had changed except my finances; the money was almost gone. I had $15.00 to my name and twenty-four hours to get out of the rooming house, or I could pay them the $15.00 for another week and starve.

THE PRICE OF REFUGE

In a small town where everyone knows other people's business, I wasn't very surprised that Milton, the custodian at the rooming house where I stayed, found out about my predicament. Milton approached me and sounded like a savior when he offered to share his nearby apartment with me for the small sum of $5.00 per week. I was so happy to pay $5.00 a week for shelter and still have $10.00 to eat with that I handed him the $5.00 immediately. When he got off work that evening, I packed my bags and he took me to his apartment. When we got there, I was totally surprised, to say the least.

First of all, it was the worst case of misrepresentation, because it was not an apartment but a little unfurnished one-bedroom shack. I had to sleep in the corner of the floor on a blanket. But that didn't bother me as much as Milton's non-stop rambling. He claimed to be an ex-soldier and, though he never told me in which country or which war he fought, he boasted about his "seven kills." When he got drunk enough, he would explain in gory detail how he performed these killings.

Late at night, Milton would dress in army fatigues, paint his face and walk around the shack with a hunting knife, seemingly stalking an invisible enemy. After the first two nights, I grew accustomed to his antics.

Maybe I should've been scared of Milton, but for some reason I was not. I pitied him and prayed for him. Each night as I prayed to God aloud so Milton could hear me, he remained quiet and not one time did he interrupt or disrespect me. I continued job hunting, but not with as much enthusiasm. I was trying to be optimistic and keep my spirits up, but it wasn't easy. There were days when I thought about Stella and a little voice reminded me that I held a return ticket to Grenada. Then I thought about my mom and remembered my promise to her. I remembered her teachings and *The Guide*, and that made me feel much better.

The week ended and Milton demanded another $5.00 from me. All I could afford was two. A few days later, he threw me out. I refused to worry about it because I believed it was in God's hands and that everything that was happening to me was a greater part of his plan. Besides, a part of me felt Milton was doing me a favor by throwing me out, because living with him was like living in an asylum.

HOMELESS, NOT HOPELESS

I now had $5.00 to my name. I was down, way down, but I was not out. I remembered my mom saying to me over and over, "When the going gets tough, you'll find out what you are really made of. Just remember, only the strong survive." She said it so often I used to think she coined the phrase.

I wandered the lonely streets of the city desperately in need of a job and a place to stay. I was crossing the bridge over the Kie River when that little voice began whispering in my ear again. "Don't be a fool, boy. Get out your return ticket and get on the first ship back to Grenada. Stella is waiting for you. Besides, let's face it, you can't even afford a decent meal, so how are you going to hitch-hike all the way to America? Stop dreaming and get real!"

I had finally had enough. I stopped dead in my tracks, covered my ears with my hands and shouted, "No! No! I am not turning back so just get the hell away from me!" People passing by were staring at me and whispering to one another. I stood there thinking for a moment, then I made a bold decision that would either save me or sink me. I took my return ticket out of my bag, held it up and said, "See, here it is, now tempt this!" and began tearing it into tiny little pieces, which I then tossed into the river. Then I said aloud, "Now you can stop trying to tempt me into turning back. It's either sink or swim."

A few people had stopped and were staring at me as if they were looking at an escaped lunatic. An elderly woman took out her rosary, crossed herself and began to pray. I just smiled at them and walked away. I was either poised under pressure or not bright enough to know when to worry.

I spent the first twenty-four hours after my eviction homeless. That night I slept on an old abandoned bus at the bus station surrounded by a few other mental or homeless people. They didn't say much and none of them accosted me. Perhaps they saw their own loneliness and despair mirrored in my eyes. The next day, I spent one dollar out of the four dollars I had left to eat, then began searching for a place to stay. Later that evening, I broke into a recently abandoned shack where I had to battle the roaches by day and large rats by night as I tried to keep from being eaten alive.

On my second day, when I returned from trying to find a dishwashing job, I was starving and spent two dollars on food. I returned to the privacy of my lonely shack moments later and ate until I was full. After dinner, I did some heavy thinking. I knew I had to come up with a solid plan and a winning hand soon. Running out of time and money, I had one dollar left to my name. I thought of my mother and wondered what she would say if she could see me now. Then I answered my own question. She would say what she had said to me at least one thousand times before: "Faith can really move mountains. Talk to God and believe he can hear you. Call his name with all your heart and he will answer your prayers."

HOPING FOR A MIRACLE

That night, I ignored the rats and roaches as I got down on my knees right there in the shack by candlelight. It felt as if God was right there with me. I called on the Almighty like never before. I said, "Father, most powerful one, if I've ever needed you, I need you now. I'm sure you can hear me and I have faith you will answer my prayers. I ask it all in Jesus' name. Amen." Needless to say, I slept like a baby that night.

I got up the next morning, washed up the best I could, took my last dollar and had a good breakfast. Then I held my head high as I went out with confidence to look for a job. I was on my last leg, but I was fearless. I was stepping out in faith. I hit Main Street and began knocking on the doors of the nightclub owners. As I was about to knock on the fourth door, a tall, thin, middle-aged black man with a frown on his face and a nasty attitude opened it, looked me up and down and said, "You have one minute to sell whatever the hell it is you're selling."

I looked at him and decided to go for broke. "Mister, I'm stranded. I just spent my last dollar on breakfast and if I don't find work today, I'll be in trouble."

His attitude softened. "What do you mean stranded? Where you come from?"

I told him my story. I told him the truth, everything. When I was through, he said nothing. He just looked at me for a good minute, deep in thought. Then he opened the door wider and said, "Come in and have a seat." He closed the door, sat opposite of me and said, "You remind me of myself almost forty years ago. I was thirteen when I ran away from home because of an abusive father. When he finally caught me, he talked my mother into putting me into a boy's industrial school, at least that's what they called it then. I spent three years in there, my mother passed away while I was in and when I came out, I was on my own."

He paused and for a minute I thought his eyes became misty. Then he continued, "I've been on my own ever since. Back then finding people to help me was harder than finding gold. So I know exactly how you feel." He stretched out his hand to me: "I am Ron Silver; this is my place."

I shook his hand, "My name is Conrad Bastien"

Then he said, "I have a little room in the back of the club where you can stay. You can sing four nights a week at the club. The pay is small, mind you, but if you are good, you will make good tips."

I breathed a sigh of relief as I jumped out of my chair and almost shook his hand off. "Thank you! Thank you! Thank you so much, Mr. Silver! You just don't know . . . thank you, sir."

He seemed embarrassed. Then he said, "Oh, one more thing. You will need to sweep up the club late at night when everyone leaves, or you can do it in the morning."

I was still thanking him. "Of course, whatever you say, sir."

He reached into a drawer, got a key and said, "Follow me!" We went to the back of the club and he opened the door to a cozy little room with a bed. After handing me the key he took out his wallet, handed me a five dollar bill and said, "Here's an advance. Go and get yourself something to eat."

I took the money, shook his hand and thanked him again as he said, "We open at nine p.m., but you probably won't be going on before eleven. I've got much to do. I'll be back around seven" And with that, he was gone.

I closed the door and as I passed by the mirror, I could hardly believe how I looked. My clothes were falling off of me. I had lost about 35 pounds. I sat on the bed, looked around my room and thought about where I had spent the last two weeks. I decided this place was the Hilton compared to the shacks I lived in for the past two weeks. I got down on my knees and thanked the Lord for answering my prayers. After showering, I went to a nearby restaurant and had a feast.

I can testify that God does answer prayers because this gig turned out to be much more than I dared to expect. It was a small club, but we got a few tourists. Some of them liked me or my singing enough to invite me to sit and talk when I came off stage each night. At times, some of them would tip me. I really enjoyed listening to the American tourists because I loved the way they talked. I loved their accents. Also, they were the most generous tippers, and I was very happy to learn that one American dollar turned out to be worth five of the island's dollars. I tried to save just about every single dollar I made.

Most of the songs I sang at the clubs were ballads like "When a Man Loves a Woman", which reminded me so much of Stella. But the tourists wanted to hear calypso, so I had to learn a few calypso songs in a hurry. At night, I often dreamt of being discovered by an American tourist, who just happened to be a talent scout on vacation, and taken back to America on a big jet plane. As the jet took off, I would look out the window at the little boats at sea and say, "There but for the grace of God go I." However, my alarm clock always brought me back to reality.

After a few weeks, Mr. Silver informed me that he had a new act coming and I had ten days to vacate the premises. That was okay because rumor had it that local singers were doing very well on the French island of Martinique. So I bought a return ticket on the ship sailing for Martinique in one week.

And so my journey continued. A journey that was as complex as it was unforgiving. This was turning out to be much more than a journey from Trinidad to America. It was a trial by fire. A testing of my fate, my spirit, and my character. It was a magical journey that seemed to be taking me from boyhood into manhood.

CHAPTER IV

I stood on the deck of the ship soaking up the hot Caribbean sun as my ship headed for the French island of Martinique. I looked way out into the distance and couldn't see land anywhere. It had been several months since I stowed away from Trinidad, and I was becoming accustomed to sailing the high seas. I leaned against the rail, looking down at the ocean and wondering how deep this part was, thinking about my life in retrospect. I looked at where I was and where I was heading; I wondered if I was on the right track. I didn't doubt myself, but questioned if I was making the right moves. Should I have stayed in Trinidad, saved enough money and then flown to the U.S.? That sounded logical, except it would have taken me a few years to save that kind of cash. Could the many people who said there's no way I could make it all the way to the United States by hitch-hiking from island to island, could they be wrong? Or were they right? Back then, it seemed logical to me—unorthodox perhaps, but certainly not impossible.

What about the ones who said, "If you're crazy enough to try a stunt like that you're not playing with a full deck." Could they be right? I was becoming confused, until I reminded myself about some of the great men I often read about in books, like the Wright Brothers, Thomas Edison and Henry Ford. I read where some folks tried to have the Wright Brothers committed when they first tried to show the world that man really could fly.

What truly inspired me was when I read that neither Henry Ford nor Thomas Edison ever finished high school, yet they became legends. That reminded me of my mom's response when I told her about Mr. Edison and Mr. Ford. She said, *The Guide,* son, those men lived by *The Guide* or they never would have made it. So study *The Guide* and live by it." I truly believe my mom was right; therefore, no matter how impossible my mission may appear to others, with the help of God, I believed I would accomplish it.

I was so deep in thought for a few minutes that I didn't even feel the scorching sun beating down on me. Now the naked parts of my body were getting sunburned, so I turned and headed back to my cabin. The next day, the sun returned with a vengeance, so I confined myself to my cabin until Martinique was in sight.

It was one p.m. as we approached the French island of Martinique, my third island in what was turning out to be the adventure of a lifetime. Slowly, the ship pulled into the bay and I could hardly contain my excitement as we began to disembark. During my time at sea, I secured enough information to know the locations of the inexpensive motels, so I got some directions and headed for them. I checked into The Merci. Though it was not the Marriot, The Merci certainly wasn't the whorehouse I had checked into when I first got to St. Vincent.

It was now two p.m. and I was anxious to get the show on the road. Martinique was a fascinating little island and I was cautiously optimistic about finding work. I had a few dollars saved from my old job in St. Vincent, but I knew that it wouldn't last me very long and that I had to find work soon. The French are such a proud race that even the poor ones seemed to possess an air of aristocracy. I admired the way they carried themselves, their sense of nobility.

NEEDLE IN THE HAYSTACK

With a list of the names and addresses of the top promoters, entertainers, clubs and hotels in Martinique, I decided to begin with the promoters. I spent the first week chasing leads. However, when I did seem to catch a break in getting on a variety show, it was only to learn that they expected me to sing in French. I knew very little French and soon began to wonder why I thought I could come here and serenade the French with songs in English. I should have done a little more research, but it was too late now.

It was the same story with each promoter. Sing in French or don't do the show. In fact, one of the promoters looked me up and down scornfully and asked, "You expect to sing in English on my show?" To him, it was an insult. My second week, I tried the hotels, thinking maybe I could get on as a lounge singer. I felt certain that the majority of the tourists spoke English, but the hotel managers, one after another, claimed their audience was mostly French and came to listen to French singers.

At the end of week two, I had crossed the promoters, hotels and lounge singers off my list of prospects. I started to get that here-we-go-again feeling in the pit of my stomach. On the bright side, I no longer heard that little voice whispering in my ear, tempting me to turn back.

Feeling a little down, I sat on the edge of my bed one night and asked myself aloud, "Did you expect this to be a piece of cake? Did you think for a minute that it was easy for any of the pioneers of not-to-long-ago who faced impossible odds, yet went on to become legends?" Talking aloud to myself was becoming a habit, but I found that it felt better when I verbalized my thoughts rather than merely thinking them. Each time I repeated a positive thought aloud, I felt as if I gave life to it.

As time went by, I was trying harder and harder to stay upbeat and positive, but it wasn't easy. During the next two weeks, I hit every major hotel in Martinique, trying to get any kind of job. Waiter. Busboy. Dishwasher. Gardener. You name it; I applied for it. The excuses I got were different, but the results were always the same. A month had gone by, and so had most of my money. I often thought of Stella, and many lonely nights I longed for her and wished she were lying next to me, telling me that everything was going to be alright. I thought I had gotten over her because I was doing such a marvelous job of trying to forget her, but every now and then, memories of her broke through and reminded me that forgetting was easier said than done.

I scratched the hotels off my list, which left only the nightclubs. I began going to the clubs, hoping they would let me perform even as a second act. However, I ran into the same problem club after club, even though at some clubs I heard French singers trying to sing calypso in English. The manager claimed their audience came to hear just the local French singers.

A manager at the Collette Nightclub who everyone called "The Fat Man" told me one night, "If you had a hit record out there, you know? If you had a name everyone recognized, that would be different." I thought to myself, If I had a name like that, would I be looking at your fat ass? Then I tried to get a job as a bouncer, janitor, anything. But it seemed that the harder I tried, the more doors were slammed in my face. In fact, it got so bad for me that I could no longer get into some of the clubs without paying, even though I was only job hunting. One night I almost got into a fight with a singer named Claude after he called me a beggar, told me to get back on the banana boat and go back to wherever I came from.

I kept trying to be cool, but it wasn't easy. I was running out of money, time and patience. I kept trying nightclub after nightclub, but still nothing. It looked like I had come to the end of the road. Visions of St. Vincent, Mad Man Milton, the shacks, the rats as big as cats, kept popping up in my mind. The very thought of having to live like that again sent shivers right through me. Normally, I prayed every night. On this night, I took my time and said a special prayer, asking God to help me overcome the obstacles that stood in my way. God was all I had, and I believed He was all I needed.

Things became so tight that I couldn't afford a decent meal each day. My rent was paid up for the next four days and after that I would have to get out. And yet something inside me kept my finger off the panic button. The fat lady was hanging around, but she hadn't sung yet.

Late that Friday night around three a.m., I was in Club Nicole waiting and trying in vain to do a song or two with the band, but they packed up and left like I wasn't even there. It was almost embarrassing, but I was past the point of embarrassment and went to sit at the bar. The club was almost empty. In the corner, a group of loud talkers sat at a table trying to out-talk each other. A guy from one of the groups was kicking the jukebox and screaming, "It keeps eating my money and not playing my song!" The bartender asked him to calm down and he flared up. Eventually, the bartender rushed out from behind the bar and, for some unknown reason, I felt I had to do something quickly.

A CHANGE IS GONNA COME

Maybe it was the frustration of the past three weeks that swept over me, but the spirit moved me. Without thinking twice, I stepped between them and held them apart at arms' length. Suddenly, I found myself singing at the top of my voice. A song I wrote a long time ago, "Will A Change Ever Come". Everyone stopped in their tracks as they stared at me in surprise. There was complete silence as I lost myself in the song.

> "I was born by the side of the river
> I grew up moving on from town to town
> I never had a place to call my home
> No one or nothing to call my own
> Oh, how I wonder will a change ever come.
> Momma died when I was just a few years old
> Then my pa disowned me, so I was told
> From then I had to be my own little man
> Cause no one cared to understand
> So now I wonder, will a change ever come.
> Sometimes, I feel like crying cause
> I just can't carry on
> Sometimes I get so tired of trying
> I sit down and wonder will a change ever come.
> Someone said, a change is gonna come
> But Lord, you know that's been so very long
> Maybe what he said was true
> But that change is too long overdue
> That's why I wonder will a change ever come.
> I can't help but wonder, will a change ever come.

I finished the song and for a few seconds there was complete silence. Then everyone began applauding and whistling. The bartender shouted, "Free drinks for everyone! This round is on the house!"

I breathed a sigh of relief as a feeling of complete exoneration swept over me. It was a damn good feeling! Finally I had gotten a chance to do what I came to this country to do. My audience was small, but they were very appreciative.

A lovely lady about twenty-four years old and looking like she lived in the gym came over, handed me some tissues, gently touched my face and told me, "Dry your eyes." I wasn't even aware I had been crying. As I took her advice, she stretched out her soft, well-manicured hand and introduced herself. "I am Sydney Duval."

I took her hand. "Conrad Bastien." She turned and waved over a heavyset man in his early forties.

"Mr. Bastien, this is my husband, Jean Duval."

I shook his hand. "It is an honor to meet you, sir."

He seemed surprised. "And why is that?"

"Because you and your group, sir, gave me the warmest reception I have received since I came to this island six weeks ago."

Mr. Duval smiled. "I find that hard to believe. You brought tears to my wife's eyes, and let me tell you, that is not an easy thing to do."

His wife extended an invitation to me. "Won't you join us . . . unless, of course, you have other plans?"

I quickly accepted and we went back to their table. Mr. Duval introduced me to his brother Jaquez and his wife Renae, then Renae's brother Mark and his wife Mandy.

Mrs.Duval turned to me. "So where are you from, Conrad?"

I answered, "Trinidad."

"What are you doing in Martinique?" Asked Mr. Duval.

I took my time and told him everything. They all listened very attentively. When I was finished, he stretched out his hand to me. As I took it I asked him, "What's this for?"

He shook his head slowly and said, "You are either a sinner or a saint." He leaned closer, "You're telling me you left Trinidad with $35.50 to your name and think you can work your way through a bunch of islands until you get to America?"

I nodded. "Yes."

Mr. Duval seemed to be genuinely astonished. "I've never met anyone with such bold confidence before. You know what? You just might be crazy enough to pull it off." Everyone at the table started laughing.

Mr.Duval studied me for a minute, then said, "I have . . ." He looked at his wife before correcting himself. "We have two night clubs in Guadeloupe. Our business vacation here ends in one week, so how would you like to fly back with us and do a two-week engagement at our clubs?" I was speechless, so he asked again, "Well, would you?"

When I finally found my voice, I said, "You're kidding me, right?"

Sydney leaned closer, "No, Conrad. We don't kid."

I looked at Mr. and Mrs. Duval. "Sure, sure I would love to, but . . ."

Mrs. Duval asked, "But what?" I was embarrassed, so I began playing with my fingers. She said, "Just say it."

"Well, I don't have any money."

Mr. Duval said, "Don't worry. We will handle everything."

A STORYBOOK ENDING

Mrs. Duval whispered something to her husband in French. He nodded, took out his wallet and handed me three brand new ten-dollar bills. "Here's an advance." He wrote something on a napkin. "And here's our phone number. We're staying at the Marriot, room 111."

I took the money and number. "Thank you both so very much. I don't know what else to say. 'Thank you' seems so . . . so inappropriate."

Mrs. Duval said, "It's enough . . . for now." I looked at her and thought I saw something in her eyes that said she wanted more, but it vanished as quickly as it came.

She was very reassuring, "Don't worry, you'll be alright. We believe in you."

I looked at both of them and said, "I won't let you down."

Mr. Duval said, as he headed to the bathroom, "I know you won't."

Mrs. Duval said, "We're going to talk to Al tomorrow and ask him why you aren't performing here nightly."

I asked her, "Who is Al?"

I saw that look in her eyes again. It stayed a little longer this time. "Oh, Al owns this club. He is a cousin of ours."

I nodded, "I see. Well, I certainly appreciate everything you guys have done for me."

"You will love it in Guadeloupe, you'll see." Mrs. Duval said.

Her husband returned and everyone got ready to leave. They gave me a ride back to my motel, where I thanked them again and promised to call the next day. When they dropped me off, it was almost dawn. After I got into my room and closed the door, I fell on my knees and thanked the Lord for rescuing me. I felt I had been taken to the very brink of a canyon, but there for the grace of God did not fall over.

At nine thirty Saturday morning, one of the managers of Club Nicole knocked on my door and offered me a paid two-night's engagement. This was the same club that told me over and over again they only hired French singers.

After he left, I sat on the edge of the bed and thought about everything that had happened to me. It truly was hard to believe. I wrote Stella to tell her I was doing fine and would be in Guadeloupe in a week, but did not send her a return address. I had gotten very little sleep the night before, but I felt wonderful.

After showering and changing, I went down to the office, straightened out my rent situation for one more week, and had a good breakfast. Rehearsals with the band were scheduled for one p.m. and I got there at twelve forty-five. The owner came over, welcomed me to Club Nicole and thanked me for stopping the fight last night. Then he told me that his cousin Sydney Duval woke him up very early this morning and told him a few good things about me. I thanked him for extending me an invitation to sing at his club and assured him I would try to live up to the build-up his cousin Sydney had given me.

Later that night, the shows went well and we had a lot of fun. The Duval's wouldn't let me pay for anything. Sydney told me she wanted me to meet her twin sister and I looked forward to it. As fate would have it, I ended up doing three nights at Club Nicole thanks to Sydney and her husband. A few days later, I took my first plane ride as we flew over to Guadeloupe to begin my two-week engagement. As my plane took off, I looked down at the boats and what appeared to be a little ship at sea. I crossed myself and began to pray, saying to myself, "There but for the grace of God go I."

I don't have a Masters' or a Bachelor's degree from a university. However, if fate could be measured or compounded and a degree awarded on its merits, I believe I would've been awarded a Doctorate.

CHAPTER V

Guadeloupe is a tropical French island that lies in the heart of the beautiful Caribbean. Its beauty is unsurpassed. The weather is gorgeous, the people are friendly, hotels are inexpensive and the food is great. The beaches, with crystal sand and clear blue water, are as pretty as a postcard. Even if you don't speak any French, you'll love it here, because most of the natives speak English.

The Duvals and I were picked up at the airport in a limousine. I was beginning to feel like a celebrity and promised myself I would work very hard with the band for the next two weeks. And who knows? Maybe those two weeks could turn into four.

IF THEY COULD SEE ME NOW

If only some of the folks who laughed at me when I was leaving home could see me now. Then another thought occurred to me. You are still a long way from the U.S. and you haven't signed a contract yet, so don't you start dreaming of signing autographs.

"Conrad? Conrad?" Mr. Duval touched my shoulder and I turned from staring out the window.

"I'm sorry."

"Man, you were very deep in thought. You were gone!"

I apologized again. "I'm sorry. I was daydreaming."

The limousine came to a stop and the chauffeur got out and opened the door for us. We were at the Eiffel Motel, a very nice looking place.

Mrs. Duval smiled at me, "Bye, Conrad. I'll see you later." I caught a glimpse of 'that look' again and was convinced it was not only in my mind.

Mr. Duval got out and said to me, "Bring your bags and come with me." I followed him into the lobby.

A well-dressed man came out from behind the counter and shook his hand warmly. "Mr. Duval, it is so good to see you."

"How you doing, Frank? How is the family?"

Frank said, "Everyone is doing well."

"Frank, this is Conrad. He will be staying with us for at least two weeks. He is my guest, so take good care of him and put everything on my bill."

Frank gave a little bow, "Yes, Mr. Duval." Then he grabbed my bags. Mr. Duval wrote something on the back of a card and handed it to me.

"Here is my home number. Call me later." We shook hands and he left. I followed Frank up to the second floor and my room.

Frank handed me the key, "If there is anything I can help you with, please call."

"Thank you." And he was gone.

I sat on the bed feeling great wishing I could see or talk to Stella or my mother. I felt a longing to share this good feeling with someone I cared about, but there was no one, so I shared it with God. "Thank you, Father, for bringing me this far. Please give me the strength to go all the way."

At this point in my life, things were going so well for me, it felt like I was dreaming. I mean, here I was staying at the nicest motel I've ever stayed in and I even had a phone in my room. I had some money saved, the rain was gone and the sun was shining down on me. So that night I got down on my knees and thanked the Lord for all the wonderful things that were happening to me. My mom had instilled in me, "If you call on the Almighty when things are going well, he'll hear you quicker than when they are going bad."

On my second day in Guadeloupe, we began to work. I was picked up at ten a.m. by Tony, the bandleader. He was a twenty three year old, tall cool guy. We stopped and had breakfast, then headed for rehearsal at the club.

Tony had a neat little five-piece band. Those guys could hold their own with anyone. We rehearsed about three hours each day and it was a breeze because the guys knew most of the songs I sang.

After practice, Tony took me around and introduced me to some of his friends, most of them in their twenties. I hoped no one would ask my age. I hated to have to lie. Posters of the upcoming show were all over town. I didn't feel right with the posters saying I was one of Trinidad's top entertainers, because I was not. However, there was nothing I could do about that except try to live up to the billing.

On the eve of the show, Mr. Duval and his wife picked me up. They had a pretty young lady with them. Her name was Shira and we all went out to dinner. Shira chatted with Mrs. Duval while Mr. Duval was busy asking me questions about my taste in women. I sometimes felt a little uncomfortable around the Duval's because I thought Mrs. Duval paid me a little too much attention. And even though he said nothing, I am sure her husband felt the same. Mrs. Duval expressed herself with her hands when she spoke to me, but when her husband was not around, she touched me even more than she should, and that troubled me.

Mrs. Duval kept telling me her sister should be back any day now from her vacation, and I wondered why she was so anxious for me to meet her.

Opening night came and the club was packed. Mrs. Duval came to the dressing room and wished everyone good luck. Before she left, she squeezed my hand and whispered, "I have a little surprise for you tonight." The sultry way she said it and the look she gave me was beginning to scare me because anyone watching would think we had something going on, and everyone knew her husband.

I wondered, is she like this with everyone? Is she trying to make her husband jealous, or is she trying to get me killed? I decided I would hurry up, find myself a lady friend and put some distance between Mrs. Duval and myself.

The show went very well. I did four songs and was called back by the nonstop applause to do two more. It was hot under those bright lights and I was soaked by the time I came off the stage, but I felt triumphant.

The Duvals seemed to know everyone, and everyone wanted to be in their company. The word must have gone out that I was looking for a lady friend, because I've never had so many females come on to me as I did that night.

A little later that evening, I got the surprise of my life when Mrs. Duval introduced me to her twin sister. I thought I was seeing double because they looked exactly alike. If they had not dressed differently, I wouldn't have been able to tell them apart. She not only looked like Mrs. Duval, she walked, talked and had the same mannerisms as Mrs. Duval. Her name was Helen, and she kept laughing at the way I kept staring at her.

ANGEL OR DEMON?

Helen was funny, smart and fun to be around. We talked for a long time and it seemed we had so much in common. She worked in real estate, but said she wrote songs and loved music. We were both single. We both lived alone. And we both loved kids and hoped to have a few some day.

There was a mystery about her. She talked with her eyes and smiled often, as if to confirm what those sexy eyes were saying. Something about the way she licked her lips, as if she were tasting something sweet.

It was time for my second appearance on stage, and Helen promised to be waiting for me when I came off. It looked like I wouldn't have to worry about Mrs. Duval in my face anymore, now that I was hanging out with her sister. The crowd was into the music and the second show went very well. When I came off stage, Helen was right there with two drinks in her hands.

She purred, "This one is yours."

I took the drink from her left hand. "What is it?"

"Piña Colada" she said.

She raised her glass. "What shall we toast to?"

I thought for a moment. "To Helen, the loveliest girl here tonight."

She laughed, "You're making me blush." And then she added, "How old are you?"

I took a quick sip of my drink and said, "Hey, you're not drinking?"

She raised her glass. "This is my third for the night. You've had one sip so far."

My ego kicked in. I couldn't let myself be outdone by a girl, so I put the glass to my mouth and drank it all in one shot.

They must have put a triple shot of brandy in my drink because one minute later, I felt like I had five drinks instead of one. I felt woozy and more daring. The band played a slow love song, so I took Helen onto the dance floor. She felt good in my arms, as if she belonged there. This girl turned me on. I hadn't been with a girl since Stella and thought to myself, if I can only get her back to my room.

The music ended and Helen took my hand. She led me to the end of the bar and ordered more drinks. I paid and we found an empty table in a corner of the room.

When the music stopped, I thought I was imagining things when Helen whispered, "My sister really likes you."

I looked at her in disbelief, then held up my glass of piña colada and examined it carefully. "Man! What the hell did you put in my drink? I think I'm hearing things."

She drew a line down my face slowly with her finger.

"You are not hearing things. You are hearing the truth."

I shook my head as if to clear it. "What did you say?"

She leaned closer, "I said, my sister really likes you."

I tried to make fun of her remark. "And I like her too . . . as a good friend. Hey, I also like her husband. They have been so good to me."

My remark did not even faze her. "Whatever my sister wants, she usually gets."

The drinks were taking a serious effect on me and I was in no mood for such a dangerous conversation, so I took Helen by the hand. "Let's dance." We headed to the floor.

Thank goodness the music was nice and slow or I would've fallen. Helen felt soft and wonderful as I held her close and whispered, "Baby, let's get out of here. Let's go to my place." She didn't answer, so I squeezed her. "Let's go to my place and finish this dance."

She looked up at me with those talking eyes. "Why?"

I was feeling my oats. "Because I want to get you alone."

She asked innocently. "You think that's a good idea?"

I playfully bit her ear. "It's an excellent idea."

"Are you under the influence?" She asked.

I kissed her. "I am under the influence of your charm." I was tired of talking, so I took her hand and said "follow me" as we headed out the door. Once outside, Helen led me to her car and off we went into the night. I was glad she didn't ask me to drive. I didn't know how.

I was not very familiar with this city, but the direction Helen was heading was not the way to my motel. Finally, she pulled up to a nice-looking house in a very nice neighborhood and said, "Here we are."

I looked around. "This doesn't look like my place."

She opened the car door. "No, it's mine." She got out of the car, took my hand and led me to her door.

ONCE IS NOT ENOUGH

As she closed the door behind us, we suddenly seemed to be at a loss for words. We stood there a good thirty seconds looking at each other, not saying a word. Then, as if on cue, we made our move at the same time. We attacked each other with an unrestrained urgency of long hot kisses and hurriedly took each other's clothes off. Fortunately, she had a rug on her living room floor because we didn't make it to the bed until forty-five minutes later. Then we started all over again because once was not enough. That was just the appetizer.

Helen's beautiful body was like a finely-tuned musical instrument and I was the new student, willing to learn, eager to play. I took my time as I slowly climbed every mountain and followed every enchanting rainbow all the way down where I explored the valley seeking the secrets to the hidden treasure. The more music I heard, the better I played until we became a never-ending symphony.

I had been with my share of girls, but Helen was a tigress straight out of Zimbabwe and she brought out the animal in me. I didn't even know I had it in me. Helen took me to school that night and taught me lessons I will never forget.

The next morning, as I lay there watching her sleep, I thought of Stella and felt guilty, as though I had cheated on her. I didn't understand the feeling of guilt because I hadn't seen or spoken to Stella in a long time. Besides, I never promised her I wouldn't sleep with other girls. I knew all this and yet I felt bad. I wished Helen was Stella, but she wasn't.

I got out of bed and headed for the shower. After Helen showered and changed, she made a big breakfast, during which she said little, but she kept smiling at me. During the trip back to my motel, we still didn't say much to each other.

The rest of the week went by like a dream. I sang four nights a week and was off three. Try as I may, I couldn't get the big smile off my face. The Duvals and their friends teased me about it and made some unprintable remarks.

Helen and I seemed to be on the same wavelength as far as a relationship was concerned. We liked each other, but didn't want to get serious because we knew it was all about the great sex. Love had nothing to do with it. We tried not to go to each other's place too often.

With a few days left before my two-week engagement ended, the Duvals took Helen and I to lunch. They told me they were in the process of forming a record company and building a recording studio. Then they offered me a thirty-day gig at their clubs. They showed me how bright my future could be and calmly suggested I consider making Guadeloupe my home.

I told them how flattered and appreciative I felt and that it was something I had to really think about. But in my heart, I knew I couldn't stay. They had been very good to me and had shown me a great time. Their offer was very tempting, especially when Helen said, "You can stay with me until we help you find your own place." It all sounded good, but I knew I didn't belong there. America was my goal, and I was determined to get there. Besides, I still felt something about the sisters just wasn't right. I couldn't put my finger on it, but I could feel it. Call it intuition, karma, vibes, sixth sense. Call it what you may, but it was there and it kept growing stronger.

Unknown to Helen, one afternoon I went to the travel agency near the dock on the bay, and bought myself a ticket on the ship leaving for St. Lucia in a few days. On the way back, I went into a church that claimed their doors were never closed and just sat there thinking. It seemed I had gone off-course; I was not as focused as I should be. I was spending too many hungry nights with Helen, when deep in my heart, I knew Stella was the only girl I really wanted and needed to be with. I told myself I was only human, but that did not make me feel any better.

Things were moving much too fast for me. I needed to get back to the basics, back to the teachings of my mother, back to *The Guide*. So I talked to God and asked Him to guide me, to forgive me and to strengthen me. I remembered the promises I made to my mother and renewed them. Then I said *The Guide* aloud as if I was saying it for my mother. When I got to the part about willpower, I repeated the meaning and considered it carefully. I left the church feeling a calm, quiet inner peace, but something was telling me it wasn't over yet.

My two-week engagement was coming to a close. Before it did, I wanted to do something nice for the Duvals, so I invited them and Helen out to dinner. During dinner, before I even had a chance to talk to them about anything, they began telling me all the reasons why I should stay here at least another few weeks. Again I lied and said I would think about it.

After an enjoyable dinner, I presented each of them with a gift as a token of my appreciation. Then we called it a night. The Duvals went home and Helen invited me to her place, but I graciously declined. I had a big day coming up and an even bigger night, because it was closing night.

My engagement at the club ended with a bang! The show was perfect. I did four songs and we were all called back onto the stage by a chorus of nonstop applause.

Then out of the crowd came the twins. They were dressed alike down to their jewelry. I was stunned because I honestly didn't know which one was Helen until she kissed me and said, "Good show."

We talked a little and then Sydney left. She was quite busy because her husband had gone away on a two-day business trip. Helen had a glow in her eyes, so I asked her, "What are you up to?"

She seemed surprised. "What are you talking about?"

"I see mischief in your eyes."

"You're seeing things," then she excused herself and went to the ladies' room.

I got a message that Sydney wanted to see me in her office, which is in the back of the club, so I went back there. As I walked in, she took a long sip of her drink and said, "Close the door." As I did, she came up to me and handed me an envelope with the rest of my pay and said in a sultry voice, "There's a lot more where that came from." Before I could respond, she stepped forward, kissed me on the mouth, and growled, "There's a lot more where that came from, too!"

I quickly stepped back and wiped the lipstick off my lips just as her brother-in-law knocked on the door and came in. I left the office all shook up, thinking to myself, this woman is sick and is trying to get me killed. Thank God my ship sails the day after tomorrow.

I decided not to tell Helen about her sister. When I met up with Helen, she noticed a change in me and kept asking, "What's wrong?"

I told her nothing was wrong, but she didn't buy it. I wondered what she would do if I told her.

A few minutes later, the show was over and the club was half empty when, to my big surprise, Sydney walked onstage with a drink in her hand, turned on the mike and made a big announcement. "Ladies and gentlemen, ladies and gentlemen, may I have your undivided attention please?" She now had everyone's attention, and most of us seemed puzzled. I mean, the show had long been over. I wondered if she was drunk. She continued to speak, "While on vacation a few weeks ago in Martinique, my husband and I had the pleasure of seeing a young man bring a song he wrote to life, without any music. Ladies and gentlemen, that young man moved me. And he is here with us tonight. I believe that if we give him a big round of applause, he will show you why I think he is destined to go places."

She was now staring at me and clapping her hands, so everyone began applauding also. I stood perfectly still, hoping it would all go away. Instead, Sydney started chanting "Conrad, Conrad" and everyone joined her. There was no escape, so I took the stage as a hush fell on the crowd. I closed my eyes for a moment and thought about my mom, Stella, my struggles, Milton and the shacks filled with rats and roaches. Then all the pain came back to me and I began singing the song I wrote "Will A Change Ever Come."

This time, before I ended the first verse, I was in tears because I was in pain. I had no desire to hide my pain, so I openly shared it with my audience.

I have never before gotten so choked up onstage. It was difficult for me to finish the song, but I did. Everyone was on their feet giving me the ovation that brought more tears. The applause lasted a good sixty seconds at least. It was such sweet agony. I stood there in tears until Helen—or was it Sydney?—came to my rescue with a big hug. It felt so good I just stood there with my head on her shoulder.

Sydney then led me off the stage. As I went through the small crowd, I noticed that a few people, including some men, were drying their eyes. Helen took some tissue and dried my eyes as Sydney kept repeating to the group of people at the table, "Didn't I tell you? Didn't I tell you this boy would move you?"

She must have read my mind, because Helen brought me my favorite drink, a piña colada. I needed it. I drank it down in two or three gulps when she brought me another. A few people stopped by my table and paid me some very warm compliments. The most interesting one came from a couple in their early fifties. They said, "That last song made the long trip worthwhile. That song alone was worth the price of the ticket."

I was now tired and tipsy and ready to go home. Helen said she was helping her sister with something, so I waited for her. Helen and I left the club about two-thirty a.m. feeling no pain. During the ride to my motel room, she was unusually quiet.

As we got to my room, Helen put on some soft music, turned down the lights and, to my surprise, opened a bottle of champagne. It wasn't necessary because the way I felt, I was wondering what was in my piña colada. And that new perfume she was wearing, man, I couldn't keep my hands off her.

DANGEROUS DECEPTION

Helen held me off by saying she had forgotten something in the car and promised to hurry back. As soon as she returned, she turned the lights down a little more and refilled our glasses with champagne. I looked at her suspiciously, "Are you trying to get me drunk?"

We both fell out with laughter and, for a second, I thought I heard her whisper "I am," but I wasn't sure. Then we both got serious and, very slowly this time, began to undress each other. It felt magical as we gazed into each other's eyes, really seeing each other for the first time. It was as if we had never touched each other before.

It wasn't raining outside, but inside it was storming and we were caught in the middle of it. I couldn't tell from which one of us the louder sound of sweet agony was coming. Our bodies pounded out a rhythm we swayed to, climbing higher and higher, more intense than a wild bushfire threatening to burn right out of control.

It was almost five a.m. when Helen woke me with a smile. She was dressed and ready to leave. The lights were bright and something was different about her. She came over, kissed me, and said, "Thanks for a night to remember. I knew it would be hot the first time I saw you in Martinique." That's when it hit me. I sprang straight up in bed as if I had been violently slapped. "Got to run now," she said. "My husband will be back today." And she was gone.

She left me speechless. That was Sydney, not Helen, I thought to myself. But how? How could this have happened? Mr. Duval has been so good to me, how can I begin to explain this to him? Will he believe me? What if he finds out? I was becoming a nervous wreck. I stayed locked in my room most of the day, not even answering the phone or going out to eat.

Thank God, my ship sails tomorrow. It was now eleven thirty p.m. and I couldn't take the hunger anymore, so I went out and got something to eat.

I got back to my room a little after midnight, and as I put the key in the door, the phone rang. It kept ringing again and again, so I answered it and to my surprise it was Helen screaming, "Get out! Get out now! Jean saw the marks on Sydney's body and she told him you forced her. He went to get his henchmen. They are coming to kill you! Get out! Get out quickly!"

I dropped the phone like it was red hot, and tried to stop my hands from shaking. I threw everything into a suitcase and two bags and got out of that motel as fast as I could. Jean Duval knew everyone in this town. I thought to myself, I will have to be very, very careful.

I took a cab and told the driver to head to the airport. After a few miles, I told him to let me out at the St. James Hotel because I had to first visit someone, so I paid him and let him go. I watched him until he was out of sight, then took another cab back to the city and got out at another motel. When that cab was out of sight, I walked two blocks and hid out in a church that stayed open, where I prayed until my ship was ready to sail the next morning.

That was the most terrifying experience of my life. It left me shaken and very apprehensive of new relationships. When that ship finally pulled out and we slowly sailed away from Guadeloupe, I gave God thanks and promised myself to never date identical twins or married women ever again.

CHAPTER VI

I was never so happy to watch an island disappear from view from the deck of a ship as I was when I could no longer see Guadeloupe. If I live to be one hundred years old, I will never understand why or how Mrs. Duval and her sister could play such a dangerous game. What if Mr. Duval and his men had caught me? The very thought of it sent shivers right through me. Thank God it was all behind me now. In three days, my ship would arrive in St. Lucia, so I needed to start finding and talking to the passengers who lived in St. Lucia to learn all I could about the country's entertainment.

The early morning sun was getting hotter, and after not getting much sleep for the past two nights, I was tired and hungry. So I got some food and went down to my cabin, where I gorged and fell asleep.

I awoke early the next morning feeling better than I had felt in a very long time. After breakfast, I spent a few hours soaking up the sun and talking to the passengers from St. Lucia, learning who the best entertainers were, and where the cheapest motels were.

Later that day, I wrote Stella two long letters. Perhaps my conscience was bothering me. Then I spent the remainder of the day writing songs.

I arrived in St. Lucia in mid-December. From what I learned on the ship, the people here loved their entertainment. I planned to stay a few weeks to put on two, maybe three shows with the help of the local entertainers of course, then sail on to Antigua, the next stop on my voyage.

Having saved most of the money I made in Martinique and Guadeloupe, I was financially okay for a few weeks. I found an inexpensive rooming house called The Damian just outside the city and paid for two weeks in advance. The people there seemed too friendly for me. By the time I checked in and settled down it was late afternoon, so I decided to get an early start the next day and went to sleep.

After breakfast the next day, I took my long list of entertainers and headed out. At the very top of this list was Ancil Fisher, manager of The Pagans, one of the hottest bands in St. Lucia. Rumor had it Ancil was a great guy with a gambling problem that was supposed to be a big secret. People said he wasn't easy to hire, but if you did get him, you had a winner.

I had pictured Ancil differently in my mind, but when I met him, he was medium height, chubby and light-skinned. Folks at my rooming house had already told me his dad was a judge and his mother a professor.

Convincing Ancil to co-produce a show with me was even more difficult than I imagined. Apparently he didn't take well to strangers. So I took him to lunch at one of the better restaurants and laid out my plans, showing him a win-win deal for us both. Then we got to talking and found out his parents were from Trinidad and might even know my parents, because they practically lived on the same side of the island. Gradually he warmed up to me and agreed to co-produce a Christmas show and dance with me. We would each put up fifty-percent of all expenses, split the profit seventy-five and twenty-five in his favor and he would pay the entertainers.

Once we had gotten the business arrangements out of the way, Ancil said, "Well, since we are going to be doing business together, I'll take you around so you can meet a few people."

I said, "Sounds good to me." We got into his shiny foreign car and off we went.

Ancil Fisher turned out to be "The Man" himself. He knew everyone and everyone seemed to love him. Wherever we stopped, the girls always seemed to be dying for his attention.

Then Ancil took me to his home. He was a bachelor living on the first floor of his parent's three-family home. His apartment was nicely furnished. He came off pretty vain as he pointed to the sign above the doorway to his bedroom that read "The Lion's Den." He sounded like a proud father as he pointed towards his king-size bed. "You have to get one of these. The girls love it." Then the smile on his face got even bigger.

During our negotiation at lunch, I saw a tough savvy businessman, but now I saw a lost little boy in search of himself. After a tour of his apartment and his soundproof basement, where his band practiced, he began making a few phone calls. A few minutes later, Ancil turned to me and said, "It's all set."

"I don't understand."

He smiled. "I've got all the entertainers we're going to need and then some. Everyone wants to sing with my band."

I was elated. "That really is good news."

He added as an afterthought, "We have the right location, too."

While riding to my rooming house, Ancil said, "We got Jamel. He's one of the best comedians in St. Lucia and we got Venus, a singing group."

After Ancil dropped me off, I thought to myself, Ancil did in minutes what would have taken me weeks to do.

For the next two weeks, Ancil got me together with his band and we did a lot of rehearsing and advertising. We were determined to make this show a success and billed it as "The Great Christmas Spectacular." Our posters were everywhere. We even got help from the newspapers. From the looks of things, I had teamed up with the right guy. Even the newspapers talked about Ancil as if he walked on water.

My nights got lonelier the closer it came to Christmas. This would be my first Christmas away from home, and the first one without my mother. It wasn't easy, but I had her memory to keep me warm. After all I had been through, I was still on track and following my dream. I think my mom would have been proud of my perseverance, which was a big piece of *The Guide*.

I was not half way there and had no idea what tomorrow would bring. Whatever it brought, I would be ready.

The boys in the band and I became very friendly. They couldn't understand how I could turn down so many invitations to party. After rehearsals, most evenings I went to my room, worked on my songs and wrote letters to Stella, but always with no return address.

Maybe I was homesick. Maybe I had become antisocial, but the invitations kept coming in and I kept turning them down. I just wanted to get on with the show and then move on.

Lots of girls were around, and some of them seemed baffled by my lack of interest. One even asked if I was gay, but after my fiasco with the twins in Guadeloupe, I was gun shy. Whatever. I decided to take it slow.

SHOW TIME

The night of the show finally came and we got a greater turnout than anyone expected. In fact, it soon became overcrowded and we had to close the doors and turn away many angry people. Ancil and I were elated.

We came to an agreement right there and then to put on another show and dance with the same entertainers on New Year's Eve, which was one week away but in a bigger hall, of course. Big dollar signs were dancing in our minds.

Finally, it was my turn to go on. I was the last singer to take the stage. Halfway through my first song, all hell broke loose at the entrance. I was tempted to stop my performance and push my way to the front door to see what had happened, but the band kept on playing and I kept on singing.

The crowd near the stage was still enjoying the show, but whatever was going on at the door seemed to be getting out of control. People were screaming at the top of their voices and then it became a stampede as pandemonium broke out, turning what started as a beautiful evening into an ugly nightmare.

It turned out that some thug to whom Ancil owed money came by with his boys to collect. Ancil and the thug got into a brawl and Ancil was stabbed. The money collected at the door was hijacked and nobody got paid that night.

During the melee, I tried to get to the door but was carried back inside by the wave of the trampling crowd. By the time I made it there, Ancil was on a stretcher being taken to an ambulance.

From that point on, I began seeing signs of insanity from almost everyone I spoke to. They were all angry with me. You would think I stabbed Ancil. They said if I hadn't come to St. Lucia, none of this would have happened.

I am sure that these same people knew all along of Ancils' gambling problem. I mean, I am a stranger and I heard the whispers, so how could they not know?

There were quite a few angry entertainers there that night. The loss was very hard on me because I had invested a lot of time and money in this project and was looking forward not only to getting my money back, but also to making some money. Half of my money was gone and so were my hopes of doing well in this town.

I just couldn't get over the way everyone was pointing their suspicious little fingers at me, saying I brought them bad luck and that's why their precious Ancil ended up in the hospital.

I wondered aloud are these folks that blind, that superstitious, or that dumb? Or could it be a little of all three? Anyway, I guess they needed a scapegoat, so why not the foreigner? Then it got worse. The next day, Ancil's family wouldn't even let me visit him in the hospital. They said I was to blame and calmly suggested I go back to wherever I came from.

I was determined to find out how Ancil was doing and refused to believe that he was blaming me for his troubles. I had to know for sure, but I wanted to hear it from him. So I hung around the hospital and waited until I saw his parents leave. Then I went up to his room. Just as I was about to enter, a deep voice called out from behind me, "You! Man, way you tink you are go?"

I turned around, "Sorry?"

This six-foot-three, gold-toothed Jamaican Rasta said, "No bother even try it! Just turn around and go way man!"

I tried to reason with him, "I only wanted . . ."

He put his hand into his pocket and smiled like ice. "Turn around, brether." He waved goodbye. "Just go while you still can." As I turned to go he said, "And let I give you a tip. If I was you, I would leave the country as fast as I can." The way he said it, the look in his eyes, that warning sent a chill through me. Finally, I got the message loud and clear. I calmly turned around and left the hospital.

Once outside, I stood there thinking, trying to figure out what the hell was really going on. I was beginning to feel that my life was in danger. I mean, nothing made sense anymore. I was confused. I headed back to my room, and to my surprise, the folks at my rooming house were giving me ugly looks and calling me dirty names. Christmas was two days away, but the spirit of Christmas around here was now on life support.

My welcome in this town was worn-out. I went down to the bay hoping to buy a ticket on the next ship leaving for Antigua in a day or two, but the next ship wasn't due to depart for Antigua before January first at ten a.m. Like it or not, I was stuck here for the next eight days.

BELIEVE IT OR NOT

I bought a ticket for January first and headed back to my room. After relaxing a few minutes, I took a long, hot shower before retiring for the night. When I came out of the shower, for a minute I thought I was in someone else's room. All of my belongings were gone. I mean everything! My suitcases, my bags, all of my clothes, my shoes, even the dirty underwear I had just taken off. Everything was gone.

I stood there naked, scratching my head. A part of me was saying, "This cannot be happening, there has to be an explanation for this. Clothes don't just vanish into thin air." But they did, with help, of course. After searching every corner of my room for the third time, finally, I decided to face reality. So I took the sheet off the bed, wrapped myself in it and headed out to the renting office.

Mysteriously, most of the tenants happened to be out of their rooms at that moment and, of course, they were rolling with laughter, especially when I asked them if they saw anyone coming out of my room with my belongings. They were high-fiving each other as if their team had just clenched a playoff spot. Everyone was having a good old time. Watching me wrapped in that white sheet was apparently the funniest thing they had ever seen.

The whole episode had an air of unreality, a nightmare that was happening to someone else. I never expected people to sink as low as stealing my clothes. I guess I underestimated their deviousness. An old man in the office took me into a back room, to a box with donated clothing. I picked out the best I could find that came close to fitting me: brown-striped pants, a yellow plaid shirt and a pair of shoes that were also a little too small for me. I was lucky to get even that.

I returned to my room and thanked God after finding my passport and return ticket where I had hidden them before taking my shower. I now wished I had hidden my money, too. My rent was due the next day.

I had a sleepless night and the next day was too ashamed to venture out dressed like a clown, so I stayed hidden away in my room. At six the following evening, Christmas Eve, I was officially evicted. As I came out of my room, the regular crowd had gathered to see me off. How did they know I would be thrown out? I looked a mess in my plaid shirt and striped high-water pants, but I held my head high. Although they had stolen my property, I still had my pride and dignity. I was not about to hide or crawl. I walked out like a man. One of the girls I had ignored since I moved in stepped up and asked, "Hey, you still think you too good to hang with me?"

Without missing a step, I looked at her defiantly and said "I am." Then made my exit. I was not about to let them see me sweat.

Hungry and homeless, but very proud of the dignified way I handled the situation, I wandered the streets in a trance-like state of mind thinking, this had to be a bad dream. I refused to believe this was really happening to me, but it was.

For the first time in my life, I was overwhelmed with a sense of desperation. Without a plan, I kept walking as if I knew exactly where I was going, even though I didn't have a clue. "Think, Conrad, think!" I was trying, but kept coming up with nothing.

Night fell and found me hungry, penniless and homeless. For the first time, I wondered if I should return to Trinidad. Then I remembered I had nothing to go back to, so I began looking for someplace to spend the night. As I walked the lonely streets, watching pedestrians hurrying to the warmth of their homes and families, I ached with a feeling of emptiness. Whenever my eyes would meet with someone, they quickly looked away and stepped up the pace as though trying to get as far away from me as possible. I smiled to myself and promised that after I arrived in America and became rich, I would go around the city at Christmas time and give a few dollars to every homeless person I saw.

UNHAPPY CHRISTMAS

It was getting late and my options were few, so I found an abandoned car with a broken window on a quiet street and got out of the chill. As the songs of Christmas carols filled the night, I found some newspapers and cardboard and tried to block the cool night air from coming through the broken window. Then it began to rain.

The sound of rain beating down on the car roof reminded me of home, so I ignored my hunger pains and pretended I was a child again at home with my mom. When I did fall into a light sleep, my growling stomach or the rain would wake me. So I said some prayers and thought about my mom until I finally fell asleep, hearing her sing one of the songs she used to lull me to sleep to so long ago.

I awoke to a quiet Christmas morning, said some prayers and did some thinking. I had to do something. I couldn't just sit there, because my hunger was becoming worse.

Try as I might, I just could not bring myself to go out begging dressed like such a clown on Christmas morning. As I was covering myself with newspaper, trying to stay warm, someone gently knocked on the car window and handed me an American five-dollar bill. I heard someone say "merry Christmas" with an American accent. I hid my face as I took the money and thanked them. As they left, I peeped out from behind my newspaper and saw a white couple in their mid-forties walking away.

Though I knew they couldn't hear me, I thanked them again before rushing off to the market to buy some food. I returned to the privacy of my abandoned car with the food and had a feast. After I ate, I felt so much better. I wished I could thank that couple face-to-face and tell them I am on my way to America and maybe I'll look them up when I got there. Then I laughed at the silly thought because I knew it probably sounded ludicrous.

I still hadn't figured out what my next move should be, so I spent Christmas day in the car. Night finally came and covered my shame as I remained hidden away from the world, hoping to wake up and find it was all just a bad dream. Unfortunately, it was reality that seemed like a bad dream. As I laid back in my temporary home thinking about this puzzle, suddenly the theory made sense. Was it a bad dream that seemed real, or was it real and seemed like a bad dream? Let's see, now, which one is it?

As I further indulged myself in my little mind game, I became fully aware that my mind was doing a wonderful job of shielding me from hurt and pain by casting a shadow of doubt on the morbid situation, instead of unquestionably accepting it as reality.

It all made sense to me. Twenty-five percent of my mind accepted it as real; however, it was so shocking that seventy-five percent of my mind hadn't totally accepted it as reality, and that created an atmosphere of hope throughout my entire being. That hope is what kept me grounded. It kept me from panicking, going insane, worrying myself to death, or doing something stupid. I had high hopes that eventually, everything was going to be all right.

SAVED

I had just finished my study of psychodrama for the evening. It was about ten p.m. and I was in the middle of Psalms 91 when someone suddenly ripped the newspaper and cardboard from the broken window, scaring the living daylights out of me. I looked up to see a tall, thin, white male in his late forties dressed in a priest vestment standing there. He stretched out his hand. "I am Father Isaac. Get up and come with me. It's too cold to be sleeping out here."

I took his hand, "I am Conrad" Father Isaac helped me get out of the car. He turned around, "Let's go."

I followed him in silence for about eight blocks to a small building behind a church. On the way there, many questions were on my mind. Does he go around the city seeking out the homeless? Is this a coincidence? Or was this my lucky day? As we entered the building, I turned to him and asked, "Father, how did you know where to find me?"

He smiled. "God knows where each and every one of his lost sheep are."

He returned from another room and handed me a washcloth, a towel and some clothes and showed me where the shower was. After I showered, Father Isaac brought me some food and we talked. I told him everything that happened to me and showed him my only remaining possessions, which were my passport and my ticket to Antigua. Father Isaac marveled at my dream of island hopping to America and seemed genuinely astonished. He said he thought it was very daring, and didn't try discouraging me.

As I got into the room Father Isaac gave me until my ship sailed, I closed the door, fell on my knees and gave God thanks for sending one of his angels to my rescue. I looked over at the bed with clean white sheets, at myself freshly showered, clean, and wearing new pajamas, and looked back in my mind at myself and where I was two hours ago.

I laid in my bed thinking. In two months I would be eighteen. Sometimes when I thought of some of the things I'd been through, I felt much older. I looked up at the ceiling fan spinning around and wondered why my life kept going from one extreme to the other. Why was my life apparently so different from the average teenager? Why was I always alone? What was I really looking for? Why was I driven to live the life of a daredevil? Was life this hard, this complicated, this lonely for all those pioneers and trailblazers I read about? The questions kept coming and coming until, at last, sleep overtook me.

The next morning, I attended a small gathering of the homeless where we all prayed and were fed. I wanted to earn my keep for the next five days, so I talked Father Isaac into giving me some daily chores. For the next few days, I went with him from eleven a.m. until six p.m. We fed the homeless at two other churches, lunch and dinner.

Between meals, I helped wash dishes, sweep floors, empty garbage and paint. Wherever I saw work to be done, I got involved.

January first finally came and I packed the few suits of clothing the priest had given me into the suitcase. Then he took me down to my ship.

I will never forget that New Year's morning for as long as I live. After I hugged and thanked Father Isaac for everything, he blessed me and wished me Godspeed on my journey. Then he handed me an envelope and said, "I hope this helps." I opened the envelope and, to my surprise, there were $200 dollars in it. I was dumbfounded and had trouble holding back the tears, so I just hugged him again, quickly turned and hurried away.

Halfway up the plank, I turned to wave to Father Isaac, and for a magical moment, my mom was standing there instead. I blinked my eyes quickly and it was the priest again. Suddenly, I felt as if I had known him my whole life. As I boarded the ship, I knew I wasn't alone on this journey.

UNBREAKABLE

There were good people in St. Lucia. I just happened to have stayed at the wrong rooming house. The demons there tried to break me. They stole all my belongings, even my underwear, but they couldn't steal my dream, my pride, determination, faith, or my will. They couldn't touch me because they couldn't steal the things that drive me. Everything they stole was replaceable.

At this point, I was even stronger and more determined, for I was unbreakable. In a few days, my ship would dock in Antigua, and whatever fate awaited me, with the help of God, I would find a way to survive.

In a way, going forward is easy when bridges behind you are burned, and there is no possible way of retreating. It's either win or die.

As my ship sailed away from St. Lucia, I stood on the deck in the morning sun and watched the island slowly disappear from view. For reasons unknown to me, I found myself in tears. Maybe the stress and all the drama of the past few weeks were taking their toll on me. Maybe I had bitten off more than I could chew. Maybe I was just tired. Whatever the reason, I just couldn't stop the tears and had no desire to stop them. To hell with being strong: tomorrow was another day. I went down to my room, got into my bed, and cried myself to sleep.

CHAPTER VII

I left St. Lucia on a local ship heading for the island of Antigua and for the next three weeks it was fun. I truly enjoyed those weeks at sea because, for the first time in a long time, I could relax and not worry about where to sleep or what to eat. Also, each island we stopped in brought me closer to my goal of reaching America.

It was a very fascinating voyage because the ship stopped sometimes for a few hours, sometimes for a day or two, at several tiny islands along the way. During one stop in Lagos, I climbed into a small boat and went ashore with a few other passengers. The island people were very family-oriented, and almost everyone was related. When I talked with the natives, I got the feeling they were speaking honestly, that every word came from the heart.

I had never before heard of some of these smaller islands and was amazed by their culture, dress code, friendliness and simple ways of life. There were some very good people on this particular island. From what I had heard, crime was almost nonexistent. The people were big on respect and every child was raised by the entire village.

As I drifted through each village and learned more about their way of life, I couldn't help but wonder, why do they stay here? How come they are not lined up at the passport office trying to get on the first boat out of here? Haven't they ever heard of America or England or France?

They all seemed to be happy. Many of the people I spoke with said they had been living here for generations and had no desire to live anywhere else. I guess we can't all think alike, but ever since I can remember I've wanted to go to America to become rich and famous. Naturally, I thought everyone did.

I told a few of the islanders that I was an entertainer touring a few of the islands on my way to America. They reacted as if I had told them I was going to the Dead Sea to walk on water. Some city folks from big countries may consider these village people backwards, but I have a feeling they can give some city people lessons when it comes to love and happiness.

I truly enjoyed the experience on each island and promised myself that someday I would return on a big luxurious ship and spend a week or two at their finest hotel.

ISLAND IN THE SUN

We finally arrived in Antigua on a quiet Sunday morning. I checked into a boarding house I could afford and, after unpacking what little I had, headed for Doctor Waterman's townhouse, the number one place on my list.

This place turned out to be a townhouse with a difference. It was a very classy joint, a combination of nightclub, restaurant, and exclusive boarding house that catered to the upper class.

Jay, the nightclub manager, told me he couldn't make me any promises, but if I came by that night, he would give me a chance to take the stage. If the audience liked me, we'd go from there.

As I was leaving the club, I ran into The Mighty Strollers, the number one singing group from Trinidad. We knew of each other from back home, but had never shared the same stage. After talking for a while, they gave me some valuable information on who to contact about a big show that would soon be taking place in Antigua.

That night, I returned to Doctor Waterman's townhouse and was given a chance to perform. Apparently, I picked the wrong night to have a lackluster performance, because I was not invited back.

I spent the next week looking for work at the other clubs and hotels, but had no luck at all. My money was getting dangerously low and I began to wonder if I should head for another island or stand and fight. Then I decided to go and see the promoter the Strollers told me about, and I got lucky. Very lucky!

He needed to replace an act for five big shows, two at the stadium and three at a nightclub. I came by just as he was about to start calling around for a soloist. I guess timing is everything.

It was about seven-thirty p.m. and I was on my way back to my rooming house as darkness slowly descended on this seedy part of town. As I turned the corner, I saw a thin, tall well-dressed guy, late twenties, wearing a red suit, black top hat, black shoes and tie and sporting a walking cane. He attacked a young girl about sixteen, almost slapping her head off her body. As she fell, he hit her with his cane, threw a handful of bills on her and shouted, "I am tired of hearing the same old shit from you. I'm short! You have fifteen minutes to bring me all my money or get the beating of your life." Then he disappeared into the building.

As I looked on, a silent rage began to build within me and I thanked God she was not related to me. I pitied her, down on all fours picking up the bills and sobbing frantically. I know I should've kept on walking, but I just couldn't. I helped her pick up the bills, then handed her my handkerchief.

"Here, dry your eyes." She dried her face and handed the kerchief back to me., "Keep it." She didn't say a word to me, but her eyes were pleading for me to help her. "I don't have much money. How short . . . . how much you owe him?"

She whispered, "Thirty dollars." Without thinking twice, I took thirty dollars out of my pocket and handed it to her.

She was suspicious, "What do you want?"

I spoke to her as if she were one of my sisters. "I want you to find yourself. I want you to get away from that monster, this neighborhood, and go back home. Go anywhere. Just get away from this life."

It reminded me of a love scene I once saw in a movie. She threw her arms around my neck and hugged me. She was crying and whispering, "Thank you, thank you, thank you." At that moment, I wanted to kill that heartless pimp.

Suddenly, there was a loud clapping in slow motion. We looked around and the pimp was standing in the doorway. "How touching," he said. Then he pretended to dry his eyes. As I looked at him, my blood ran cold.

The young woman whispered to me, "Don't! Just go, please go!"

I touched her face gently. "Take care of yourself." She nodded and I walked away, never looking back. I was halfway home when it dawned on me; I didn't even know her name.

When I got home, I had a long talk with myself and promised to try harder to mind my own business. Then I placed the incident behind me and got back to concentrating on my mission at hand.

I gave the Almighty a lot of thanks that night because someone, somewhere, was looking out for me in more ways than one. Rehearsals began the next day and the first show opened in one week. Then I began to wonder about the next time. I kept coming close to the edge, sometimes even hanging over before being rescued. What if my luck ran out?

IN RETROSPECT

I had a lot of trouble falling asleep that night, so I just lay on my bed and reflected on my whole life. Where I came from and where I was trying to go. I wondered silently, am I heading in the right direction? My thoughts were flowing. I tried in vain to stop them. In a few days I would be eighteen and felt I should be closer to my goal. What was I doing wrong? Was I just a dreamer? Was I aiming too high? Would I ever get to America?

Sometimes I felt certain I was on the right track, that I was doing the right thing. Every now and then, however, I had my doubts and America seemed like light years away. I thought about my mother and the aunts who raised me, all the countless sacrifices they made for me and all the trouble I put them through. I felt sure that, if they weren't in Heaven, they were on their way.

So far I had been to ten different islands, five of which I had performed in. Ten islands were now behind me and I had about nineteen more to go. I lay there wondering what fate awaited me on those islands ahead. And then finally, thank God, I fell asleep.

A few days later, the stadium crowds were much larger than any for whom I had ever performed. For the first few minutes, I was severely intimidated. Once I settled down, I did just fine. It didn't take long for me to get the crowd on my side and have them singing along with me. The show was a success and my confidence grew.

Two days later, when the much smaller crowd at the nightclub got rough, I went into the audience and sang to the ladies. It worked very well and I collected more tips than I had in quite a while.

On the day I turned eighteen, I kept it to myself. I did a little celebrating with Jill, a lovely lady friend I met backstage after the show at the stadium a few nights before. She was the sister of the bandleader. We shared a wonderful night together at her place. During small talk as we lay in bed the morning after, she said she was recently separated and would soon be filing for a divorce. That got me very upset because when we first met, she told me she was single.

I got out of Jill's bed, showered and began dressing in a hurry as she tried to explain herself. I calmly told her, "I do not date married women."

The following night was closing night at the club. We had a good turnout and did a great show. When I came off stage, Jill was there trying to explain. I quickly lied to her and told her I was with someone, and she left me alone. That's when I literally bumped into Monique, or did she bump into me? Anyway, to put some distance between Jill and myself, I allowed myself to be seduced by the charms of Monique, who kept praising my performance on stage.

Monique looked like a model and seemed to know many people. We found a place at the end of the bar and I ordered two piña coladas after she claimed it was her favorite drink, also.

We talked for a while and seemed to have a few things in common. There was something intriguing about her. She sounded older and more experienced than someone in her early twenties. Or were my eighteen years beginning to show?

After some more small talk, Monique invited me back to her place, which she said was only five blocks away. Over in the corner, some guy was in deep conversation with Jill, who kept staring at me. If I didn't know better, I would say she looked very worried.

We were on our third drink when Monique again suggested we go to her place. I thought why not? After all, this was a night to celebrate. Why not let myself live a little? However, I insisted we go back to my place, which was even closer, and she agreed. We walked to my place and got there around four-thirty a.m. By this time I was really feeling those drinks, but I was also wanted a shower. When we got to my room, I stripped and headed for the shower. Monique promised to join me shortly.

The cool water felt good on my skin, and I began humming "Crazy," a Patsy Cline song. The shows at the night club were a big success, but what really surprised me was when James, the promoter, not only paid me something extra, but also handed me a plane ticket to beautiful Barbados in a few days to do four shows.

For the first time since leaving Trinidad, I felt as if I really was on my way. It was such a great feeling. I felt I belonged in this business of shows and entertainment. Suddenly, New York didn't seem so far away. A few more shows on a few more islands. How difficult could that be?

Happy days were here at last. In my mind, I saw myself stepping off a jet at Kennedy Airport, kissing the ground and saying, "Thank you, Jesus." But first I had a few more islands to go through.

I turned off the shower and began drying myself. I decided to pay my rent, buy some new clothes and stash the rest of my dough. That's when I remembered Monique was supposed to join me.

I called out to her, "Hey Monique! Monique!" I came out looking for her. "Where are you hiding?" I looked in the closet, even under the bed. The room was empty. She was gone. Something told me to check my pockets. I didn't have to; they were turned inside out. I sobered up in a hurry, threw on some clothes and dashed downstairs, looking up and down the street. Monique was nowhere in sight. I told myself, come daylight, I was going to find her.

On the way back to my room, I punched the front door so hard that I injured my hand as part of the wood broke. I was going to find her if I had to search the whole damn city.

I had just gotten paid for the shows and had well over $400 dollars in my pocket. Luckily, I got into the habit of hiding my important papers and some money in a secret place in my room. I checked it and found my passport, ticket and $150 dollars. I breathed a small sigh of relief.

I lay across the bed wanting to kick myself for trusting that little ... I thought of the names I wanted to call her, and of my mother, so I dropped the dirty names.

I didn't plan on falling asleep, but I did and woke up four-thirty in the afternoon. At five p.m., I hit the streets and began looking for Monique. She said she lived five blocks from the club, so I started in the east and began working my way to the west.

Three hours later, I was still searching with no end in sight. I talked to several people and described her to them, but no one seemed to know a Monique who fitted that description. I decided to keep looking.

It was almost nine p.m. and I was getting tired, so I decided to call it a day. Without thinking, I found myself passing through the same block that the 'Monster

Pimp' beat the young girl on a few days ago. I was almost halfway into the block when a car pulled up ahead of me and, to my delightful surprise, Miss Monique and two other girls got out. That very same pimp walked up to the three young ladies. They were so full of themselves that neither of them noticed me.

Each of the girls handed the pimp a fat wad of cash. He whispered something to them and they headed back to the car. I ran up to Monique. "Remember me? I want the money you stole from me right now!"

She smiled as if she was onstage and pointed to her colorful pimp. "Ask Slim. He has your money."

The pimp walked over to me. "Why you bothering my ladies, chump?" We were face-to-face.

"She stole my money and I am not leaving here without it!"

He turned to the girls. "Get in the car and get out of here. I'll take care of this fool." As I tried to get Monique, he hit me from behind with his walking stick and then pushed me to the ground. The girls sped away in the car.

As I got to my feet, the pimp took off his jacket, grabbed his walking stick in both hands and said, "Yeah, I got your money. Come and take it from me, sucker."

I approached him very cautiously. "Why don't you put down the stick and fight me like a man, you batty boy!"

That really pissed him off. He stepped to me, eyes blazing, and violently swung his cane toward my head. I blocked it with my left hand and instantly countered with a well-timed right cross to his jaw. Muhammad Ali, Joe Frasier and George Foreman would have been proud of me. It was such a beautiful shot. Slim's eyes rolled back, he went limp and fell like a brick. I hesitated briefly, then went into his pockets and emptied them. He wasn't moving. I'm not sure he was even breathing.

Out of nowhere came the young girl I gave the thirty dollars to a few days ago. She grabbed my hand. "Hurry! Let's get out of here!" I looked at the pimp; he still hadn't moved a muscle. A crowd was gathering as she tugged on my hand. "Please! We must hurry. Let's go!"

The young woman led me through some alleys and back roads until we came to a small room in the back of a house. Once inside, she grabbed a suitcase and began packing in a hurry. "What are you doing?" I asked.

She answered without slowing down. "They saw me lead you away. They will be looking for both of us. You have to move, too. Slim knows everyone in this town."

I took out the stacks of cash I stole from the pimp and counted it. To my pleasant surprise, it came up to almost $1,200 dollars. I gave her half. "Here is $600 dollars. I hope this helps you get out of here."

She hugged me. "I'm getting out of the country and going back to St. Vincent on the first plane I can catch. What about you?"

"I'm flying to Barbados in two days."

"Good!" She said. "My aunt will put us up for two days. Let's go to your place and get your stuff." I told her the address and once again she led me through alleys and back roads I would never have found on my own.

Once at my place, she stayed outside to get a cab while I ran in, packed and returned in a flash.

She agreed with me, so we changed cabs three times before getting to her aunt's house. Her aunt drove us to her sister's house near the airport. Her aunts were very accommodating and didn't ask too many questions. They both thanked me for saving their niece and were happy we would both be out of the country in two days.

The next day, her aunt took us to the airport. The first thing I did was buy a newspaper, where I learned that the pimp was alive but hospitalized for a few days with a broken jaw and a concussion.

The story read: "Pimps at war, fighting each other over girls and territory." We had a good laugh and were happy to know that the law was not after us.

In a way, I hated to see her leave and knew I would miss her. I looked at her like a little sister. I had no romantic interest in girls my own age or younger. Her plane was boarding, so I hugged her, kissed her on the cheek and waved good-bye.

The next morning, her aunt brought me to the airport and I quickly boarded the plane to Barbados. And as my plane took off, I remembered that I forgot to ask her name.

CHAPTER VIII

It was midday and my plane was about to land at Barbados Airport. From the air, this beautiful island looked like one big tropical flatland, filled with trees dressed in their autumn leaves.

I took a bus from the airport and with a little help from the passengers found an inexpensive motel and checked in.

There was a carnival atmosphere about this island unlike any other I had visited. Calypso and steel drum music could be heard everywhere. The smell of spices and Bajan cooking hung in the air like a subliminal invitation. Most of the locals were dressed in bright colors, wore bright smiles and walked in rhythm as if they were about to start doing the limbo any minute.

Barbados is the home of some of the top entertainers in the Caribbean, such as The Merrymen and Jackie Opel, who many thought were in the same class as James Brown. I was looking forward to sharing the stage with these legends. I knew that this big event was going to be covered by the news media from a few different countries. If I did very well, I would be in the newspapers of a few countries. Maybe it would be in Grenada's papers and Stella would see it.

Anxiety kept me awake much of the night and I was the first one to arrive at the theatre, where the artists were supposed to meet the promoter at eleven a.m. I felt like a child on his first trip to Disney World must feel. With so many top guns here, I would probably be limited to singing two songs. My plan was first to sing "When a Man Loves a Woman" and one of my own compositions, "Will a Change Ever Come."

Time went by and everyone was there except the promoter. We assumed he was running late. Then the entire day went by before we got word that he had had a heart attack on his way to the airport this morning and was in the hospital. The show would have to be postponed for two weeks.

HERE WE GO AGAIN

When I first heard the news, I felt as if I had just been violently punched in the stomach. It took the air right out of my sails. I had trouble breathing. I had to hang on or I would fall. I told myself not to worry, it was just a postponement, but a voice inside my head said, that's what you think! Regardless of all the positive things I was telling myself day after day, I started getting a bad feeling in the pit of my stomach.

Waiting was the hardest part. The days went by very slowly and I tried to get some work at one of the nightclubs, but had no luck. I began to feel as if the bottom was beginning to fall out in slow motion. "Stop it!" I commanded myself. I had to stop the flow of negative thoughts that were running through my mind. I had to change my way of thinking. So I kept my fingers crossed and prayed that the promoter would get well soon and the show would go on as scheduled. But my sixth sense told me it was not meant to be. The days crawled by, each one slower than the one before, and I tried my best to keep a positive attitude.

At the end of the second week, we got the news I instinctively knew was coming. The show had been postponed indefinitely. On top of all that, I either misplaced or lost a fifty-dollar bill. Either way, my funds were very low, and my spirits were even lower. Then the rain that was threatening all morning began coming down with a vengeance, but I refused to give in. I forced myself to keep two job appointments. They did not work out and I was still out of work, running out of money and now soaked.

I was caught in the rain literally and figuratively. After a while, I stopped trying to dodge it. I just walked in the rain and let it beat down on me. Depression was knocking very loudly at my door, saying something about an "overdue appearance." I was doing my best to ignore its seductions, but after listening to the wrong voices in my head, I decided to do something I had never done before. I bought a bottle of rum, a bottle of coke, went up to my room and started drinking. Alone.

I was tired of everything and wanted to run away, to hide away from the world. As the heavy rains tried to claw their way into my room, I stayed hidden and drowned my sorrows.

I stood outside myself and looked at me, saying this is not the Conrad I know. This is a weakling, an imposter. Shut up! Just shut up! I shouted. My next-door neighbors were probably wondering, if I had company or if I was losing it?

My rent was due in three days, but I just didn't seem to care. My mind was tired and I didn't have the will to try to figure a way out of my calamity. It felt as if it was raining all over the world. Outside, the winds picked up and it seemed more like a storm or a hurricane. How appropriate, I thought to myself. As day turned into night again, I stayed hidden away with my demons. I glanced out the window and parts of the city seemed to be in darkness. This must be the storm they were predicting all week. I hadn't eaten in over twenty-four hours, but I wasn't hungry. I had my rum.

Later that night, the wind rattled the windows and one flew open. As I staggered over to shut the window, the strong wind blew the Bible and the half bottle of rum off the edge of the dresser. The bottle rolled on top of the open Bible. I crawled over, picked up the bottle and was about to pick up the Bible when my eyes were drawn to the big letters at the very top of the page. The Bible had fallen open to PSALMS 130, which happened to be one of my mom's favorites. It was one she used to say aloud many times a day, seven days a week. This was one of several psalms I grew up on and knew by heart, so I began reading it.

I closed my eyes as I said it out loud, just like my mom had taught me. "Out of the depths have I cried unto thee, O Lord. Lord, hear my voice. Let thine ear be attentive to the voice of my supplication."

When I finished Psalms 130, I was directed to recite the 91st Psalm, another one of my mom's favorite. "He that dwelleth in the secret places of the most high shall abide under the shadow of the Almighty." And for a peaceful moment, I was a child again. My mom had her arm around me as she said the 91st Psalm with me. I was in her arms and unafraid. Then the winds died down and the rain ceased.

When I got through praying, I felt at peace with the world. I knew I wasn't alone. Very calmly, I got up and emptied the remainder of the rum into the sink, took a shower and went to bed. I didn't worry about tomorrow; in fact, I didn't worry about a thing and believed that by the grace of God everything was going to be alright.

I don't believe in ghost stories, but for as long as I live, I will always believe my mom was there with me that night in my room.

I was up and out early the next morning and spent most of the day looking for work without any success. I went to the Marriott Hotel, the last place on my list. My interview with assistant manager Mr. Napoli, was going so well, I even told him about my financial dilemma. It just so happened that a bus boy position was available, but two dishwashers had just quit and he desperately needed a four to twelve o'clock dishwasher. I volunteered to work as a bus boy from 8-4 and a dishwasher from 4-12 six days a week if he could help me out with an advance or a place to stay.

Mr. Napoli said there was a small room near the laundry I could stay in as long as I was working both shifts. To him, he was getting a good deal if I really could do both jobs. To me, it was a small price to pay. This gave me a chance to save some quick money by working two jobs and not having to pay for food or rent. This was a blessing in disguise.

I couldn't believe my luck. However, a small voice inside my head was saying, something somewhere wasn't right. I ignored the warning. I returned to my motel, packed my things and moved into the small room at the Marriott the same evening. I wrote Stella and was tempted to send her my new address, but something told me not to.

My first week of employment was a breeze. Working sixteen hours a day did not even faze me, especially since I didn't have to travel to get to either job. I made a few phone calls daily and kept in touch with the other entertainers to find out how Big Barry was doing and when the show would be rescheduled.

Barry was still in the hospital and that was all anyone knew. So I threw myself into my job and saved as much money as I possibly could. Another two weeks went by that were like the first one. I had no life except work and sleep, but I didn't mind. I was saving my money and I was happy.

As time went by, I began to notice a change in Mr. Napoli, he became a little too friendly. His hand lingered on my shoulder and he always gave me a little squeeze when he spoke to me. And if no one was around, he came up a little too close to me when we were speaking. At first, I found it amusing and said to myself, No way! It's impossible. You are jumping to conclusions. His touching became much more frequent.

HIS TRUE COLORS

About eleven one night, Mr. Napoli called me to his room saying it was very important. He met me at the door half-naked, with blood shot eyes and smelling of alcohol and offered me a drink. I refused and only sat down after he insisted. Mr. Napoli came and sat too close to me, put his arms around me and tried to kiss me. I sprang out of the chair and screamed at him as I headed for the door. "You are a sick man and you are drunk! Good night!"

Mr. Napoli ran and blocked the door as he said, "Where do you think you're going?" Then he grabbed my private parts.

I almost lost it! I pushed him away with such force that he flew halfway across the room and fell. I stepped to him screaming, "Do I look like a batty boy to you?" He became sober in a hurry as he got up, apologizing over and over again and begging me to keep my voice down.

The more he pleaded for me to be quiet, the louder I screamed obscenities. It was all I could do to stop myself from hurting him. When I told him I was going to tell the general manager and everyone at work tomorrow, he ran to a drawer and pulled out a brown bag. I thought it was a gun and my heart began to race even faster.

He was in tears as he shoved it to me, pleading. "Please, please don't do that. You'll ruin me. Here, take the money." I hesitated and wondered how much money was in the bag. He quickly added, "I'll get you some more tomorrow. Please! How much will it take to make you forget this ever happened and just go away?"

I felt sorry for him, but also felt I should not look a gift horse in the mouth. I counted the money in the bag; it was $250. I told him that with another $250, I could be out of the country in a day or two and he agreed. I thought about turning down the money, but only for a brief moment. This was a gift from somewhere, and although I was not proud of the way it came about, I was not about to throw it all away. I picked up $250 from him the next day and quickly bought a ticket on a ship sailing to Jamaica.

I felt like a cat that kept landing on its feet and believed it was more than luck that kept me surviving and overcoming obstacles. It had something to do with my never-say-die, positive mental attitude.

CHAPTER IX

I was in such a rush to get out of Barbados that I ended up getting on the wrong ship to Jamaica. The one I got on was smaller and it was the local that made stops at every little island between Barbados and Jamaica. By the time I realized my mistake it was too late, so I decided to relax and enjoy it.

My ship stopped for a full day, sometimes for two days, after reaching each tiny island. As a result, a trip that would normally take one week on a bigger ship going directly to Jamaica would now take three, maybe four weeks.

These tiny islands could not accommodate the ship, so it remained a half mile from shore. The passengers and cargo would then be transported to and from shore by boats.

I enjoyed traveling through those islands and was always one of the first ones to get on the boat that took the passengers to shore. The different cultures, customs and ways of life on these smaller islands never ceased to amaze me. Never had I imagined there were so many tiny peaceful little islands tucked away in the heart of the Caribbean. After the first week, I was tired of visiting every island we stopped at, so I remained on the ship for the rest of the trip.

I had a lot of time on my hands. I wrote new songs, worked on the old ones and made friends with some folks who lived in Jamaica. I needed to learn all I could about this land they called Jamaica. I heard it was the toughest, meanest of all the Caribbean Islands, but there were good opportunities for talented entertainers. I was warned to stay away from certain neighborhoods and that there were a lot of bad ones. To me, that was not exactly news because I felt certain that every country had its share of good and bad neighborhoods.

Jamaica has a long list of internationally known entertainers, such as Bob Marley and the Wailers, Byron Lee and the Dragonares, Toosh, and Hopeton Lewis and the Heptones, to name a few. I sat there enjoying the sun and thinking to myself, it would be nice if I could get on a nationally-broadcast show with all these top guns. I quickly said to myself, "You've been sitting out in the sun too long," and I got up and headed down to my cabin.

We finally sailed into Kingston Harbour after a few weeks at sea. I was well rested, had some money saved, and was ready. After clearing customs, I called the number to a rooming house that came highly recommended. It had good rates and was in a good neighborhood. The folks on the phone at the rooming house told me they had vacancies, so I got directions and headed out to catch a bus to Kingston Eight.

WELCOME TO JAMAICA

I looked around me and thought, so this is the Jamaica I have heard so much about. I could hardly believe I was really here. I was really excited to be in Kingston town, home of Harry Bellafonte.

I had a great feeling about this town. Maybe all my troubles were behind me. If things went just right for me, who knew? I could soon make enough money to buy a plane ticket to Puerto Rico. Man! That would be so exciting, I thought to myself as I hurried to catch the bus. I stepped off the curb and almost got run over by a truck I never saw coming. God only knows how I survived that fateful moment. An angel must have been watching over me, stopping me in my tracks as the truck sped by. It came so close to me the air pressure almost knocked me over, and the driver didn't even blow his horn or slow down.

I stood there trembling as my heart tried to beat its way out of my chest. I watched in disbelief as the truck quickly disappeared from view. A bold sign right in front of me read, "Welcome to Jamaica."

After calming myself down, I caught the bus and traveled forty minutes to the boarding house. It was a very large, private home divided into rooms with private baths and kitchens.

After settling in, I got the newspaper and began checking out the local talent. I spent the first two weeks going to different nightclubs, looking for a chance to perform. I also attended variety shows, trying hard to make some kind of connection, only to discover that hundreds, if not thousands, were also making the rounds of the clubs and the showcases looking for that lucky break.

I felt disappointed and had no idea why, probably because I had never been exposed to such tough competition before. The countries I had been to were less than half the size of Jamaica, but so was the competition.

What really worried me was the fact that some of the talent I had seen was so much more polished than me. It made me wonder. If the guys who live here can shine like they do and still not get picked up by a promoter or recording company, then what are my chances of getting lucky?

I stepped back and asked myself what made me think it would be easy? Did I think I was one of a select, few people with talent out here trying to make it? I thought if the competition in Jamaica was rough, wait until you get to America and you'll see what stiff competition really is.

What was it that my mom used to say about when the going gets tough? Anyway, I kept plugging away, hitting the clubs, the showcases and the variety shows. I followed every lead and every rumor, refusing to let anything hold me back or hold me down. My mom told me I was different. I was unique. There was only one me. So I didn't care if there were ten-thousand other singers out there searching with me. I was going to get mine.

I was now into my third week. There were so many nightclubs all over Kingston. I felt something had to give, and soon. So persistence became my password. Every rejection I got, I smiled because I felt sure it brought me one step closer to that "yes" I would eventually get.

One Saturday night, a club manager really burst my bubble when he turned me down and said, "Singers here are a dime a dozen. You would be lucky if any club would let you sing, even for free."

That was a major blow to the head that sent me reeling. It really hurt. I staggered over to the bar and ordered a piña colada. I drank it in two or three long sips, and then headed out at one forty-five a.m. After waiting thirty-five minutes I caught the bus for home. I must have been more tired than I thought and that drink didn't help. I fell asleep and missed my stop by about two miles, so I got off the bus and started walking back.

NIGHTMARE CITY

It was now three a.m. The streets were deserted, the last bus had just left, and I couldn't find a taxi. I guess this was not their favorite neighborhood late at night. So I began walking home. After a few blocks, I looked around and thought I shouldn't be caught dead walking in this neighborhood in broad daylight, much less at three a.m. But I had to get home.

I followed what I thought was the same route the bus had taken, but it didn't look familiar. I came up to a convenience store that looked like it sold whatever was convenient for the boys in the hood, but they told me they were closed and slammed the window shut before I could ask a question.

On the side of the store were a group of guys sitting around a fire, smoking a strange-smelling, over-sized cigarette and passing it around. They had long, braided, matted hair that looked like soap, water, or a comb hadn't been near it in years. A giant rasta sat in the middle of the group. He wore a black t-shirt that matched his skin and his red eyes. His t-shirt read in big red letters: SATAN.

I got directions from them and an ice-cold stare from the giant with red eyes. I remember thinking to myself, all he needed was a pitch fork, a tail, and a pair of horns protruding from his forehead. I stepped up the pace after leaving those guys because I began having a funny feeling I was being followed. I didn't see anyone behind me; it was just a feeling, so I walked a little faster. Then I turned a sharp corner and ran right into Satan himself.

He was about 6 feet 6 inches, two-hundred fifty pounds. He didn't have horns or a fork, but he did look like the devil. He was dressed in black and pointed a big gun at my face. I froze. Before I could think of something to say, I felt the cold barrel of another gun pressed against the back of my neck. I just knew this was the end of the road for me.

The guy behind me said in a heavy Jamaican accent, "If you want to live, man, don't turn around."

Satan in front of me reached in, grabbed my bag, then said very slowly, "Take off your watch, your shirt, your pants and your shoes man. Hurry!"

My heart was pounding so loudly, I felt sure they heard it. Did he say my pants, too? I wasn't about to ask any questions, so I took off everything except my underwear. My fingers were trembling so badly I had trouble unbuttoning my shirt. I finished undressing and, as I handed Satan my belongings, I felt something warm running down my legs and realized I had urinated on myself. I began to pray aloud because, with two guns to my head, I thought I was as good as dead.

Satan lowered his gun and started laughing showing a mouthful of broken, yellow teeth. The guy behind me removed the gun from my neck and said, "Way you from, man?"

I had trouble finding my voice. "Tri . . . Trini . . . Trinidad."

He laughed out loud. "No worry bredda. Dis you lucky day. My grandmamma is from Trinidad." Then he asked me, "Can you run?" I started to turn around to answer him, but I remembered his warning. I tried to say "yes" but no words came out, so I nodded instead. "Good. When I say go, I want you to run, man. And don't look back. Just run as fast as you can." He tapped my shoulder. "Now go!"

When that man said "go," it was like I was in the Olympics, the world was watching, and my country's last chance for a gold medal rested on my shoulders. I sprinted away in my wet drawers, picked up speed after the first block, and ran the fastest half-mile I ever ran. Then I collapsed.

I couldn't catch my breath. Each time I stood up, my knees buckled and I fell again. I was on the sidewalk at three a.m. crawling around on all fours like a dog, but I was alive so I didn't care. I wasn't even ashamed.

I tried to stop several vehicles, but they all sped up. I crawled to a few houses before I found someone with a phone who was willing to call the police for me. When the cops finally showed up, they had a hard time looking at me and keeping a straight face. They gave me a sheet to cover myself, and after I told them what happened, they no longer thought it was a laughing matter. They said I was lucky to be alive.

After refusing medical attention and an invitation to come to the station to look at mug shots, I was taken to my rooming house. My landlord was not happy that I had to wake him up at four in the morning. He was less happy when he heard I had lost his keys and my money. He never once asked me what happened or if I was alright.

When I finally got into my room and closed the door behind me, I leaned against the door and slowly slumped to the floor. Still wrapped in the sheet, I got into a fetal position and began rocking myself. Everything kept replaying in my mind. I could still see Satan's face and his mouthful of broken, yellow teeth when he smiled. Something was happening to me, but I had no idea what it was. Feeling numb and unable to concentrate on a plan of action, I just wanted to lie there on the floor and rock myself away from everything.

I have no idea how long I remained on the floor before getting up, showering, and getting in the bed. My rent was paid up for a week and I had $40 dollars, my passport, and return ticket well hidden in my room.

I tried to put the incident behind me, but I couldn't. The emotional scar went deeper than I thought. For two days, I wouldn't leave my house and had no interest in anything. Every sudden noise I heard, especially after dark, rattled me. For two days, I gave serious thought to getting on the next ship and making my way back to Stella. I longed for her to hold me and revive me. I longed to hear her voice. Maybe then this nightmare would end. I was still seeing my life flashing before my eyes. I thought about my mother, but I needed to be in Stella's arms.

When I was aboard the ship, I heard some bad stories about Kingston, but I thought that bad things only happened to other people.

By the third day, I somehow felt stronger and managed to talk myself into staying. However, an uphill battle awaited me because my rent would be due in a few days and still no job was in sight. Cautiously, I spent the rest of the week checking out clubs and showcases that were closer to home. I made sure I got home earlier and stayed wide-awake on the bus ride at night.

SAVIOR OR SLICKSTER

Rumor had it that La Coury Record Company in Kingston paid cash if they really liked your songs. I was in desperate need of cash, so I made my way over there. Placing my cards on the table, I told them I was interested in getting my songs recorded and getting a cash advance. They assured me I had come to the right place.

An hour later, two of my songs were on tape with the help of Jackie, one of the best piano players in Jamaica. There was one problem; the producers loved my music and the beat to my songs, but not the lyrics. The name of my song was "The Screw" and I was talking about a new dance. This version was too clean for them. The producers said it wouldn't sell and wanted dirty, suggestive lyrics, so I sat down and in less than an hour I rewrote the lyrics for both songs.

They loved it. We kept the same rock steady beat and the same melody. We named the new songs "The Screw, Part One and Two."

Everyone felt we were going to have a hit record. In fact, they were so impressed they decided I should meet the boss, Mr. La Coury, himself.

Mr. La Coury was a short, stocky, overweight man in his early fifties. He looked biracial and smoked a fat, funky smelling cigar. Mr. La Coury got up from behind his cluttered desk and enthusiastically extended his hand to me. "They tell me you could be the next big thing here in Jamaica. Something about a new dance called 'The Screw.'"

I shook his hand. "I hope they're right, sir."

Mr. La Coury laughed, "They tell me you changed the lyrics from clean to dirty in less than an hour. That's impressive."

"Well, sir, I need the money, so I had to do it their way."

Mr. La Coury threw his arm around my shoulder. "I like your attitude. Let me tell you something, son. We're one big family here. If you become a member of this family, you can go places. The sky is the limit. We can make all your dreams come true."

I turned to him. "How do I become a member of this family, sir?"

"It's very simple: have faith in us. Put yourself in our hands and we'll do the rest."

I thought to myself, man, this guy is saying all the things I want to hear. This must be my lucky day.

Mr. La Coury didn't like my real name. "From today, your name is 'Falcon Price.' That is the name we will release your new single under."

I agreed. "Whatever you say, Mr. La Coury."

My new single. I could hardly believe it! The producers rolled out the red carpet for me, offering me champagne, a contract and a cash advance. Everything was coming at me so fast it made me dizzy. Like a well-rehearsed play, everyone was telling me how talented and lucky I was. Suddenly Jennifer, a very lovely eighteen-year-old some said was Mr. La Coury's daughter, offered me her phone number and asked me to call her soon.

Mr. LaCoury's staff came at me from every side. Then Mr. La Coury called me into his office and told me he had a check and a contract for me. He poured me another glass of champagne and told me, "This is a chance of a lifetime, son, but this contract has to be signed today. Right now. The studio musicians are standing by, waiting to start work on your record." Then he pushed me over the edge. "Remember, this check is only a small advance. Tomorrow, when everything is wrapped up, you'll get a much bigger check." Then he poured me some more champagne.

I thought what the hell? So I asked, "Where do I sign?"

That made him very happy. He handed me a check for $50 dollars, which he cashed, then shook my hands and assured me. "This is only the beginning, the tip of the iceberg." Then he asked me where I was staying. I told him, and he shook my hands again and had his driver take me home. Sitting in the back seat of that big car, I felt I had made the right decision.

I got to the recording studio bright and early the next morning. A few minutes later, the musicians arrived and we got an early start rehearsing both of my songs. We rehearsed until we got it right, then we all took a break.

When we returned from Mr. La Coury's office, we settled down and did three takes of my songs. The first time I heard myself with the band behind me on those big speakers was a moment I would never forget. As I listened, I wished Stella or my mom were there to hear it. They would have been so proud of me. I wished they would release the record under my real name instead of Falcon Price, but I didn't have much say in the matter.

After making the record, still walking on air, I went to see Mr. La Coury so I could get the rest of my money. His assistants told me he would be away for a few days, so I asked to see Jake, another one of Mr. La Coury's assistants. I kept getting dumb excuses. When I got tired of the excuses, I barged into Jake's office and demanded an explanation. Very calmly, Jake handed me a copy of the papers I had signed in a hurry yesterday. It turned out I had signed away all the rights to my songs for $50 dollars.

I felt sick. I had to lean on Jake's desk to keep from passing out. I was speechless. Jake sat there looking at me with pity. "Are you alright?"

I couldn't find the right word, so I nodded. Then I broke the silence. "How is this possible? How could they steal my dreams, my hope, and my life so easily? How could I one day be lifted up to the top of the world and the next day be brutally slammed to the ground, head first, by people who looked me in the eye, shook my hand and lied to me?"

Jake got up from behind his desk, calmly looked at his watch, then looked at me and said, "Welcome to the wonderful world of show business."

I followed him out of his office and he quickly disappeared down the hall. I tried to talk to a few others, but everyone was late for something. They all claimed to be busy. The same people who yesterday were pressuring me to sign the contract while pouring me another glass of champagne were the same ones who were now avoiding me. And all Jake had to say was "welcome to the wonderful world of show business."

Eventually, I left the La Coury Recording studio, but I knew in my heart it wasn't over. In fact, it was far from over. I wasn't going to take this lying down. I had to do something, I just didn't know what that something was as of yet. Sometimes, when it rains it really pours. When I got home, I faced an even bigger problem. I was behind on my rent, so my landlord had padlocked my door. After pleading with him, I gave him $40 of my last $50 dollars, but that bought me only one night. I would have to come up with another fifty by ten a.m. or check out.

Once again, it seemed I had come to the end of the road. Maybe I should write a play and name it "Up The Creek," then star in it. I wouldn't have to act. I could just be myself.

I called the ship harbor's office and found out there was a ship leaving the next day for Barbados. After all, I did have a return ticket. I decided that would be my last resort. In the meantime, I would try to come up with something. But try as I may, I came up with nothing.

I stayed awake all night worrying. When morning came, my only option was to get on the ship and head for home. So I packed my things, took a bus to Kingston Harbour and got on board. Coincidentally, my ship was passing through Grenada on its way to Trinidad, its final stop. How ironic? I thought to myself. Could I have come full circle?

WHICH WAY IS UP

Maybe faith was playing tricks on me, building me up only to watch me fail again. Testing me to see how much I could take. I sat there remembering the promise to my mom just as they began making the last call for all non-passengers to disembark. I had about forty seconds to decide . . . going or staying . . . now or never. Then a voice in my head said, "Get your ass off this ship right now!"

I grabbed my bags and hurried off. I had barely gotten off when they began taking up the plank. Why did I get off? What was I going to do now? Did I have a plan? You would think that I did, but I didn't. I just knew that any move I made would be better than giving up and going back home.

I stood on the dock watching the ship as it slowly made its way out to sea without me. Then I turned and tried not to look like a foreigner as I wandered the lonely streets of Kingston. Was I a glutton for punishment? Why did I keep ending up in a corner with my back against the wall? Did I have a death wish? What would I do? Where would I go? Could I be afflicted with a mild case of insanity and not be aware of it?

As night fell I kept moving, trying to look like I knew where I was going. It was getting late when I found a broken down bus on a quiet street and sneaked inside to spend the night. Before falling asleep, I said the 91st Psalm and refused to worry myself to death.

The next morning an idea hit me like a ton of bricks. Trinidad's number one entertainer, The Mighty Sparrow, for whom I auditioned before I left home, had told me that he was a good friend of **Ronnie Nasralla**, who had an office in Kingston. Ronnie happened to be the manager of Byron Lee and the Dragonares, Jamaica's number-one band.

I called information and got Ronnie's phone number and address, cleaned myself up and walked across town to his office. Mr. Ronnie Nasralla was a warm, wonderful gentleman in his early thirties who happened to be white and had a heavy Jamaican accent. I told him I was a singer-songwriter, a friend of The Mighty Sparrow (I stretched the truth) and was stranded there after being robbed at gunpoint. Unfortunately, this was the truth.

After listening attentively, Mr. Nasralla picked up his phone, made two phone calls and one hour later I was in a very nice rooming house thirty minutes from Kingston. The room and board was paid for one month in advance.

After calling and thanking Mr. Nasralla, I sat on my bed feeling so grateful and confused as tears rolled down my face. Why was God so good to me? Why did he keep rescuing me and saving me from myself? I was no saint, not even a good guy, and I never pretended to be one. What had I done to deserve such blessings?

I was just getting over my feelings of gratitude when a young girl knocked on my door and told me lunch was ready.

For the next few weeks, my life was a Cinderella story. Ronnie got me together with Byron Lee and the Dragonares, and I was fortunate that Mr. Lee could add me to his list of singers for his next few upcoming shows.

When I first met the band, I was shocked because I expected them to look like the typical Jamaicans. They did not. Except for two black guys, the other ten members of the band were Chinese-Jamaican. When you looked at them, you saw Chinese. When you heard them speak, you knew they were Jamaican born and bred.

I had a great time with these guys. They showed me how the upper class lived. I met many interesting people and attended a few very nice parties. But as a singer, I wasn't knocking them dead.

I had to make a decision, so I decided that after this month I would say goodbye to Jamaica and move on. Byron Lee had enough good singers in his band. He was only doing me a favor in the name of Ronnie and Sparrow, and I was not about to wear out my welcome. Before I left Jamaica, however, I had a little score to settle with Mr. La Coury and his bandit record company.

I hatched a plan I knew would work well because it catered to their greed. For several days before I vanished, I showed everyone I came in contact with what they thought was really a plane ticket back to Trinidad, leaving within a few days. I told everyone I was going back home. That is the trail I wanted anyone looking for me to follow. I did not intend to underestimate Mr. La Coury.

Later that same day, I went back to La Coury record company and offered them ten songs for $600. After haggling back and forth, I ended up putting twelve of what they believed to be my songs on tape and got $450 with the promise of another $450 after the songs were recorded. Then we shook hands, hugged and made out like one big happy family before I left.

The very next day, I got on a ship and sailed away from Jamaica. Two days later, when my ship made a pit stop at a small island, I called La Coury record company and very calmly informed them that they had been duped.

Those twelve songs they paid me $450 dollars for were not my songs, but songs recorded in other countries by other well-known artists. I also told Mr. La Coury to tell his assistant Jake that I said, "Welcome to the wonderful world of show business."

When Mr. La Coury finally spoke, he sounded as if he was having a coronary and mumbled something. I hung up on him because I didn't want to hear anything he had to say.

Somehow I didn't feel a great deal of satisfaction and couldn't help but wonder how many other poor songwriters had put their hearts, souls and dreams into their songs, only to have them ripped away by this ungodly predator. What I did was wrong, but I figured it was time for someone to make Mr. La Coury and company victims of their own devices.

CHAPTER X

The next stop my ship made was in Antigua, where my plans were to get off and take a plane to St. Kitts. Earlier research showed St. Kitts was not far from St. Martin or the U.S. Virgin Islands. I was headed in the right direction.

For the next few days, I lay around the deck of the ship and enjoyed the summer. I wrote Stella, wrote a new song, and sang a few of the old ones. I stood on the deck of the ship, looking out to sea, reflecting on my life. It seemed a lifetime ago that I stowed away and began hitch-hiking my way to America. Almost two years later, I was well past the halfway point and wondered what lay ahead.

I remembered how important it was to my mom that I understood the importance of God and *The Guide* in my life. Now I understood clearly what her objectives were, and she was so right. It's quite obvious to me now why she called the principles *The Guide*, because without desire, faith, willpower, discipline, perseverance, pride, and dignity, I never would have made it this far.

My ship sailed into Antigua on a hot July morning. After a series of phone calls, I was lucky enough to get a seat on a plane flying to St. Kitts in four hours. I had time to kill, so I got a newspaper, had a long breakfast, and did a little window-shopping before heading out to the airport.

Instead of finding the bus, I treated myself and sprang for a cab to the airport. I picked up my ticket, got a magazine and settled down to wait until we started boarding.

My flight was uneventful except for the talkative lady who sat next to me. My plane landed in St. Kitts at four p.m. and I caught a ride into town with that very same lady.

After checking into an inexpensive rooming house, I took my list of contacts and headed out to make some phone calls. St. Kitts was a small island filled with warm, friendly people. After what I went through a few weeks ago in Jamaica, I found St. Kitts to be a refreshing change.

I had very little trouble locating Lester, the number one guy on my list who was said to be one of the top soloists in the country. Lester was nineteen, 5'10, one hundred and fifty pounds and considered himself a "chick magnet." Lester was a friendly, playful guy who told me that I got there just in time, because he was doing two shows the following weekend. Since his elder brother Carl was the promoter, he was sure he could get me on.

Lester took me across town and we met Carl. At nineteen, Lester was six years younger than Carl, but looking at them, one would think they were twins. Lester told his brother I was a friend of his, and with a handshake from Carl, I was on.

Over the next two days, Lester took me around and introduced me to members of his band and a few of his friends. We spent the rest of the week rehearsing.

I was a little surprised at how laid back the people of this island were. Nothing seemed to bother or excite them. Everyone seemed to know everyone else and, like most small communities, almost everyone was related in some way.

The weekend came and it was show time. But I just didn't get that feeling of excitement from anyone. The crowd was smaller than expected and the show did all right, but something seemed to be missing.

After the show, Lester felt it was necessary to apologize to me for such a low turnout. But I was not surprised by the small crowd because there had been very little advertising. One good thing did come out of all this, and that was that Lester and I became friends. We clicked and understood each other so much. He felt like a brother to me and invited me to go to the small island of Nevis with him in one week to do a big show. Of course, I accepted.

When I asked Lester about the hotel rates in Nevis, he said, "Forget the hotels and motels. We're staying with my aunt. She has a big house and it's just her and her daughter." So we hung out in St. Kitts a few days more, then caught a small plane that looked and flew like a model plane that scared the living daylights out of me until we landed safely in Nevis.

I hadn't heard much about Nevis and would have to say it was one of the Caribbean's best-kept secrets. It had everything one would want in a tropical island, plus it was not crowded.

We stayed with Lester's Aunt May and her lovely twenty-year-old daughter, Beth. He wasn't kidding when he said her house was big. His aunt and cousin treated me like I was a member of their family.

Lester got me into all three shows that he was already booked for. We also got a two-weekend engagement at Club Brazil.

As the days flew by, Beth and I became friends. The first thing I did was explain to her, in front of her mother, that I was "passing through" and had one objective in mind, and that was getting to America to become a rich and famous singer-songwriter. Her mother seemed to like me. She called me the most honest boy she knew. She said Beth was in college there but hated it, so she was trying to get accepted to a college in New York. That sounded wonderful to me.

The weeks flew by much too quickly and I hated leaving. However, during the last show here in Nevis, I met a promoter named Jessie and agreed to go to Montserrat to be on his show in five days. I invited Lester, but he had a previous engagement back in St. Kitts and had to decline.

The day of my departure came and I thanked Lester and Aunt May for their overwhelming hospitality. Beth took me down to my ship and I kissed her so long before boarding the ship to Montserrat. She stood there waving as they pulled up the steps in preparation for departure and I thought to myself, it was fun and she is a very nice girl, but there is only one Stella.

By now, I was accustomed to the ships stopping at smaller islands along the way, so this time I just skipped most of them. I looked forward to doing the show in Montserrat and wished Lester had decided to join me. I knew nothing about Montserrat and wondered what it was like there.

It was about five p.m. when my ship pulled into the port of Montserrat. To my surprise, I was met by Jessie, the 30-year-old promoter I met in Nevis who was promoting the show here in Montserrat.

I went over and extended my hand to him. "It's nice of you to meet me, Jessie."

His handshake was weak and he spoke with no conviction in his voice, almost timidly. "I'm glad you came." He took both my bags. "Is this all your luggage?"

I tried to make a joke of his question. "Yes. I travel light."

TOO GOOD TO BE TRUE

Jesse turned and pointed. "I'm parked out in the front. Just follow me." I followed him thinking to myself why does he seem so shy, almost afraid? Why does he avoid eye contact when he talks to me? And how is it he didn't appear this nervous when he approached me to appear on his show the first time I met him in Nevis?

We got to his jeep, he unlocked the doors and threw my bags in. I asked him, "Where can I find an inexpensive motel?"

Jesse seemed very surprised. "You don't have to stay at a motel, you can stay with us."

"You mean you and your wife?"

He smiled for the first time, "I'm not married. I live in Cannabis with my parents."

"Are you sure they won't mind? I mean, this is kind of sudden."

Jesse spoke with confidence for the first time. "They won't mind at all. They can't wait to ea . . . I mean meet you."

I looked at him puzzled. Did he say *eat* or *meet*? He quickly added, "We only live a few minutes away. It's not too far from here."

I thought to myself, this is a chance to save the motel money. On the other hand, this does seem too good to be true.

Jesse saw my hesitation and asked me quite calmly, "Is something wrong?"

"No, I was just day dreaming." We got in the truck and headed for Cannabis.

We soon left the city behind us and headed north on a bumpy dirt road that led into some kind of a forest. Sensing my uneasiness, Jesse said reassuringly, "It's just on the other side of this plantation." The road was rough and we had to drive slowly, but after a while of seeing no street signs, houses, or even signs of life, I began to wonder just where the hell we were, and what was really going on.

I was trying to figure out this puzzle, but more than one of the pieces was missing. So I decided to give Jesse a few more minutes as the sun was setting and darkness was approaching. We seemed to be going deeper and deeper into a jungle. I felt sure something wasn't right, so I asked, "I thought you said your place was not far away?" He turned to me with a cold smile, but said nothing. That's when I knew I was in trouble.

Just then the truck rolled over something and got a flat tire. Jesse turned off the engine as we got out of the truck to check. The first thing I heard was the silence. It was dead quiet. Too quiet. No singing birds, humming bees or blowing breezes. The leaves on the trees didn't move and everything stood still. It was as if a silent audience was watching, but holding its breath.

Then we noticed we had not one, but two flat tires. I held my head as I looked first at the darkness sneaking up on us, then at Jesse. He didn't seem to be worried. He just stood there wearing a cold, silly grin as if he knew something I didn't. Then the thought hit me. I could be dealing with a nut or maybe even a serial killer. How on earth did I allow myself to get this deep into the jungle before deciding to do something? How come I didn't see this coming? Me, who was supposed to be so damned perceptive.

I wasn't far from panicking as I asked, "What are we going to do?" Jesse put his hands in his pockets and shrugged his shoulders. At that moment, I thought I saw a pair of eyes watching from behind a big leaf. I looked closer, but saw nothing. Then I thought I heard a noise as if someone had stepped on a twig. Again I looked around, but saw nothing. However, when the hairs on the back of my neck stood up, I took a closer look at those leaves and this time saw a few pairs of eyes watching me, unless I was losing my mind.

THE GREAT ESCAPE

I knew I had to be very cool and keep my composure, so I told myself calmly, very slowly, turn and face the direction in which you came. Now, if you want to live, run! Run like the wind!

I took off as if I heard the sound of a race starter's gun. As I sprinted away, I heard a harsh command from a deep voice in a language I did not recognize, and the race was on. After a few hundred feet, I picked up even more speed.

Fear can do that to a person. In some cases, fear can paralyze you, or it can give you wings.

As a child back home, I walked and ran a few miles to and from school each day. So if there was one thing I was good at, it was running. This time I believed it saved my life. I didn't look back or slow down to see who or what was chasing me. I just ran like hell for a good mile and a half until I reached civilization. Then I ran some more.

I didn't stop running until I knocked over a few people as I flew through the doors of a filling station, scaring everyone in sight. The attendant called the cops, then the ambulance, because I looked like hell and, when I tried to speak, nothing came out. I had lost my voice and my legs were so weak I fell each time I tried to stand.

Later at the hospital where I was admitted, when I stopped shaking and finally regained my voice, I told the police what happened. They told me how lucky I was to be alive. "Cannabis is a place no one goes. It's where the Cannibals live; that's why they call it Cannabis." They claimed that over the years, a few people went there and were never seen or heard from again.

I told them of the oversized pot I saw hanging over the firewood as I sped through a village and they said, "Body parts are boiled or stewed in the large pot."

I quickly covered my ears and closed my eyes. I thought I was going to be sick. My mind was in turmoil as I turned to the nurse. "Cannibalism cannot be happening this day and age. It's just not possible."

She was calm. "Ok. So tell me, who or what do you think was chasing you?"

My body trembled as I tried not to recall. "I don't know. I only saw the eyes and, I think, painted faces."

She smiled playfully. "Would you care to take another trip to Cannabis?" This conversation was giving me the creeps.

I made the sign of the cross across my chest. "Can we talk about this tomorrow, in the daytime?"

She felt victorious. "Ok." She began taking my temperature and fell silent.

After I described Jessie, the promoter who drove me up there, the police said, "he was insane" and started laughing as they told me the whole story. "Jessie was born and raised in Cannabis with his parents, who are cannibals, until he was nine. Something happened and his mother fell out of grace with her people and reverted. She then brought Jessie to town and never went back. A few years ago, Jessie's dad, who still lives in Cannabis, put a curse on his mother and she went insane and killed herself. After that, Jessie lost his mind. Before his mother's death, he co-produced a few shows and, in his mind, he is still producing shows. He is the only person who goes back and forth to Cannabis untouched and unafraid. The unsuspecting strangers he takes up there are never seen or heard from again."

Hours after hearing the horror stories, I couldn't sleep. After two days in the hospital, I still didn't get much sleep and had no appetite, so the doctors kept me another few days. I called the office at the harbor and there was a ship leaving for St. Martin in three days, so I talked my doctor into releasing me in time to catch it.

Before leaving the hospital that morning, I tried to talk to my doctor, Stan Nomas, a native of Montserrat, about the cannibals. He looked at me like I had three heads and said indignantly, "I do not know what you're talking about." Then hurried away. Dr. Nomas looked back as if to see if I was following. I found his behavior to be very strange.

Thank God I still had my money and passport. Everything else was lost. I left the hospital wearing donated clothes that didn't fit me well, but at this point how I looked was the least of my concerns. I bought a ticket to St. Martin and waited nine hours before my ship sailed.

While waiting, I did a little shopping close by, replacing everything that was left on Jessie's truck. It was ten-thirty a.m. I was in the city looking around, but I was still freaking out. I examined the faces of the people around me, perhaps to see if any of them favored Jessie. Then a silly thought came to me. What if a few of these people around me are really cannibals dressed as regular everyday folk? Stop it, Conrad! Just stop it! You're being ridiculous! Oh, am I really? Is it impossible? You're going to drive yourself insane if you don't hurry up and get the hell off of this island. You know what? I agree with you.

The lady standing next to me turned to me with a puzzled look. "What are we agreeing on?"

I was totally surprised. "I'm sorry?"

She smiled as though we knew each other. "You said to me that you agreed with me. I wanted to know about what?"

I held my head in disbelief. "Oh my goodness! I am so sorry! I was just thinking out loud."

Her smile got brighter. That's when I noticed how lovely she was. She waved her hand. "That's alright. I do that sometimes myself." Her brown blouse brought out the brown in her eyes. She was about twenty-eight, 5'9", one hundred and twenty-five pounds, long beautiful black hair and a smile that was as bright as the sun.

I was just about to introduce myself when her husband came up and said hello. We said our goodbyes and I came back to reality and headed back to the seaport. On the way there, I bought a magazine and something to eat.

We finally boarded the ship and I was a very happy man. When the ship began to slowly sail away from Montserrat, I made the sign of the cross, thanked the Almighty for saving me, and promised myself to never ever go back to Montserrat for as long as I live.

CHAPTER XI

SSome say motivation is just an emotion. If there were ways to market motivation, and put it into drug stores all across the nation, a much larger number of people would be successful. At age eighteen, this was a revelation to me. When I looked back on some of my close escapes on some of the islands, they scared the daylights out of me. And yet I was so motivated to get to America that I was prepared to face the Devil in Hell. Turning back was not an option, because I had nothing to go back to, also because my mind was made up. I was on a mission.

After leaving the nightmare in Montserrat behind, I slept for two days straight. And now, here I was on the deck of a ship taking me to St. Martin. The warm September breeze caressed my face in the early morning sun as I listened to the singing of the waves and the seagulls above me singing their sweet song of Thanksgiving.

I looked out into the distance where the sea seemed to meet the sky and a big smile came to my face. St. Martin. St. John. St. Thomas. Puerto Rico. That's four more islands, then New York. I felt like dancing and had to contain the excitement that was quickly building inside me. You are close, but you have a long way to go, I told myself. Don't relax, but don't get too anxious. Stay focused and determined and you'll be alright.

I had left my home in Trinidad well over one year before and had passed through about twenty-five different islands so far. Looking back on some of the obstacles I overcame and how close I was to my goal, my heartbeat quickened with pure excitement.

We were scheduled to arrive in St. Martin in a few days. Having spent last Christmas in an abandoned car, I couldn't help but wonder on which of these islands Christmas would find me. I prayed this Christmas would be much better than the last one.

I spent my time at sea daydreaming about New York and talking to a few passengers who lived in St. Martin, trying to learn all I could about that island

and the U.S Virgin islands. The more stories I listened to from people who claimed they had been to America, the more excited I became about getting there. However, St. Martin was next.

The morning sun was just rising as we approached the island. St. Martin is truly a fascinating little island. It's like being in two different countries at the same time, because one side of the island is French and the other side is Spanish. A huge mountain separates one side from the other.

I caught a bus to the Spanish side because I learned that the rent and many other things were less expensive there. I checked into a rooming house and paid two weeks in advance. This rooming house was not bad and it was practically on the beach.

I walked on the beach, especially at sunset and watched the sun slowly go down. It left me feeling like a lonely stranger on the shore. I wondered what Stella was doing. Was she thinking about me, too? I wished I knew.

For the next two weeks, I traveled to and from the French side in search of a job at the nightclubs, but found none. So I began looking for any kind of job I could find. I had four islands to go before getting to New York. I was superbly inspired and nothing could bring me down. My confidence was growing.

ANGELS IN DISGUISE

Then the third week came and I struck gold in a most unusual way. I was out walking a few blocks from my rooming house when I passed a tourist couple trying to change a flat tire. I had never before changed a flat tire, but something made me turn around and offer my help.

I walked over and introduced myself. "Hi. My name is Conrad Bastien. Looks like you could use some help with that tire."

The man took my hand. "I am David Bradley and this is my wife, Cathryn." I shook her hand and bowed. He pointed to the tire. "Do you think you can get it off?"

"Sure. If you show me how." David looked puzzled.

"Have you changed one of these before?"

"No. This will be my first."

He looked at his wife and they both laughed. She said, "I like his attitude."

"Well, thank you, ma'am," I said as I bowed to her.

For the next twenty minutes, I followed David's instructions until I successfully changed my first flat tire. They thanked me and offered me some money, which I turned down. We talked a while and I told them of my journey. Where I came from. How I got here. Where I was headed. They seemed amazed.

Then David handed me his card and said, "If you are ever on the French side and need anything, please come see me. We own the Marriott, the number one hotel on the island."

My ears perked up like a rabbit's. "You're kidding me, right?"

They both replied at the same time. "No, we're not." They looked at each other and smiled; only they knew what their smiles meant.

Half-jokingly, I said to David, "I could use a job."

"What do you do besides entertain? And when can you start?"

I replied, "I am a waiter and I can start immediately." I quickly added, "I am also a busboy and a dishwasher. If there's work to be done, I can do it."

The Bradleys turned out to be angels in disguise. They drove me back to my rooming house, waited for me while I packed up my things, and then took me to their hotel.

When we got to the Marriott, it amazed me how the workers ran after them to take their packages and catered to their every need. David called over one of the managers and said to him, "Sam, this is Conrad, a friend of ours. He will be with us for a few months, maybe longer. Please put him in room 000. And Sam, tell Herman I said Conrad can start in the dining room as a waiter the day after tomorrow." He turned to me, "This will give you some time to settle in." He and his wife shook my hand again. "If you need anything, just let Sam know. He is our general manager."

LIVING A DREAM

It was like something I once read about in a novel or magazine, but never for a moment thought would happen to me. It took me quite a few days before I believed the turn my life had taken. My first few weeks at work, I felt as if I was living a dream. All of my co-workers seemed to be going out of their way to help me. One would have thought my last name was Bradley.

I have never enjoyed a job as much as this one. I felt I ought to be paying them. Over several weeks, I came to know some of the single female guests quite well. I turned down invitations to stop by their rooms for drinks when I got off work because I felt that would be against hotel regulations. It would also be a betrayal of the trust the Bradleys had in me, and that was something I would never do.

However, when I suggested to one of my lady friends that she come to my room and she came, that was a different story. On a few occasions, the other waiters couldn't figure out why some days I wore such a big smile, but the waitresses did. To me, women are far more perceptive than men.

I tried to be very discrete and not have company too often, but it wasn't easy. For a while, I lived the life some guys only dreamt about. It was difficult, but I often reminded myself why I was here and what my goals were.

Saving money was my number one priority. Number two was gathering information about the US Virgin Islands, Puerto Rico, and America. Many of the tourists were American, so that gave me the chance to learn more. Very seldom would I take a day off because, to me, that wasn't work.

The weeks flew by, Christmas came and, thanks to the Bradleys, my co-workers, and Ann, a guest I met, I had one of the best Christmases I have ever had. However, as soon as the crowd left and I was alone, loneliness engulfed me. I missed my mom and Stella terribly.

When New Year's arrived, a green light began blinking in my mind and I knew the time had come for me to move on. I had saved all of my money, gotten valuable information, and was ready. So I thanked Mr. and Mrs. Bradley, my co-workers, and my lady-friends, and got on a ship heading for the Virgin Island of St. John. Leaving was a little difficult because I loved my job and new friends. Every day and night was fun and that was great, but I wanted so much more.

For two days and nights, we sailed and enjoyed the endless ocean view as we headed for St. John. Something was telling me instead of stopping over in St. John, I should go directly to Puerto Rico. However, my research had shown that January to early April it is winter in New York. The thought of cold weather scared me, so I decided to stay with my original plan and go to St. John.

I spent a week in St John, where I tried to find a job and could not. Of course, I would be dishonest if I said I tried hard to get a job there. The truth is that discipline kept me job hunting for at least one week, because that was part of my plan and I did not intend to deviate. At the end of the week, I got on a ship heading to St. Croix.

I spent two weeks in St. Croix and yes, I did try a little harder to get a job there. I came close at least twice, but things fell through. Perhaps it was because I had good money saved from St. Martin and did not give job hunting my all. Then again, St. Thomas was calling me. I did go to quite a few of the clubs in St. Croix, but each of them said they had all of the singers they needed and then some. So I headed over to St. Thomas.

The nightlife in St. Thomas was more exciting than any of the other Virgin Islands. I spent a week there and wasn't surprised that I didn't get a job because I had a glimpse of the kind of competition that awaited me in New York. Some of the singers I saw were very good. I had one consolation: I wrote my own songs, so if I didn't make it as a singer, I would make it as a songwriter.

I didn't sing at the clubs I visited in St. Thomas, but I truly enjoyed some of the shows. It seemed like every club I visited, a singer was performing James Brown's "I'm Black and I'm Proud," or it was playing on a jukebox.

Anxiety was getting the best of me and after a week, I couldn't take it any longer. I got on a ship and sailed over to Puerto Rico, my final stop before America. I knew it would be difficult for me because I spoke no Spanish, but I refused to see that as a handicap. I was so excited that even if the people there spoke Chinese, I would still find a way to get a job, save some more money, and then go to New York.

I was on such a high from knowing how close I was to New York that nothing could bring me down. I was so close to it I could taste it. I felt driven, motivated, and determined. I had God and *The Guide* on my side, just like my mother had taught. I was ready.

CHAPTER XII

I stood on the deck, deep in thought as my ship approached the island of Puerto Rico, the last of twenty-nine islands I had to work my way through in order to accomplish my mission of getting to America. I reflected on the life-and-death struggles I endured on some of the islands I visited and felt that whatever fate awaited me in Puerto Rico could not be any worse.

Even though the sun was shining, it began to rain lightly as my ship pulled into the bay in Puerto Rico. As we slowly came off the ship, I looked up and saw the largest, most beautiful rainbow I had ever seen. I stood there for a moment and watched as the sun came through the rainbow, shining in all its glory. And I believed there was a message for me way up there in that beautiful sky. Something was telling me that I was close to the end of my very own rainbow, and that thought gave me a wonderful feeling. My journey was far from over, but the end was now in sight.

I wasn't very far from New York and the anxiety of getting there was threatening to get out of control. I had to cool it and focus on Puerto Rico, on getting a job, saving more money and learning even more about New York.

I found a cab driver who spoke English and asked him to take me to the Salvation Army shelter in San Juan. After telling the folks at the shelter my situation, they agreed to let me stay there until I got on my feet. I wished I had known about the Salvation Army twenty-eight islands ago.

I spent my first week in Puerto Rico job-hunting mostly in San Juan. Finding a job there was not as easy as I thought it would be. I found myself thinking of Stella more than I usually did. For some unknown reason, I wrote her, gave her my address and asked her to write to me. Then I kept the letter a few weeks before mailing it.

My limited knowledge of the Spanish language was a major stumbling block during my search for a job. It was an obstacle I had to find a way to overcome. The comical reaction I sometimes got from prospective employers when they learned I didn't speak Spanish amazed me. I guess non-speaking Spanish folks just didn't job hunt in Puerto Rico.

After dinner at the shelter most evenings, I would hang around and listen as small groups of older men would talk about their younger days in America. Each of them had a different story for what brought them to the shelter. They all loved to talk, and I enjoyed listening to them because I learned so much. I would ask one person a question about New York and instantly get four answers from four different guys. Each of the men claimed to know the most about New York City. I was very excited about this thing called snow. It sounded fascinating . . . little white pieces of clouds falling from the sky. I had never seen snow before and was looking forward to seeing it.

I enjoyed these little meetings, but some evenings I was so tired after job-hunting all day that I just stayed in my room and had an early evening. The most important piece of information I got from those guys was to find an American girl and get married if I want to become a US citizen. I made a note to put that at the very top of my list of things to do when I got to New York.

Night after night, I prayed to God a little more, asking for his help in finding a job before my money disappeared. Another week went by and still no job was in sight. Out of desperation, I bought a Spanish newspaper and had a man at the shelter translate the want ads for me. I had to talk him into it because he felt sure I would be wasting my time.

I wrote down some phone numbers and called a few of them. Most of the people I called hung up on me when I couldn't reply to them in Spanish. The next day, with some help, I got the name and address of a hotel where they needed dishwashers, then took a bus and went to the Flamingo Hotel in the town of Rio Pierdras. This was a thirty-five minute bus ride from San Juan.

At my job interview, the manager and his assistants had a good laugh when they realized I didn't speak Spanish and couldn't reply to their questions. I was getting a little tired of the cat-and-mouse game. After all, it was only a dishwashing job. So when the assistant manager, who spoke very good English, asked me my name, I brazenly told him to tell the manager, "I came here to work very hard, not talk very much." He translated and there was silence as everyone looked at the manager, who was looking at me very thoughtfully. Then I gave him the push he needed. I stepped up to the translator and said to him, "Translate this. Let me work for you today for free. If you like my work, then hire me tomorrow." His assistant translated, there was a moment of silence, then the manager stretched out his hand and, as I firmly shook it, I knew we had a deal. I began washing dishes that day as if my life depended on it, and was sent the next day to obtain a social security card. When I returned with it, he hired me permanently.

For the next few weeks, I was the hardest working and happiest dishwasher in Rio Pierdras. I got along so well with my co-workers that they started teaching me Spanish. The hotel fed us well and, except for transportation, I saved most of the money I made.

MY FIRST SON

I got home one evening and found a letter from Stella under my door. As I opened the letter, a picture fell out. I picked up the picture and looked at it as my hands began to tremble. It was a picture of a beautiful baby boy just over one year old. For a moment, I was looking at a picture of myself seventeen years ago.

I read the letter and learned what I instinctively knew. I had a son. His name was Kenny. I became so excited that I bolted out of my room to show the picture to the entire group and to shout to everyone who would listen, "I have a son! I have a son!"

I made a complete fool of myself, but didn't care. I just wanted everyone to see my new son's picture. I stayed awake half of the night admiring my new baby boy, writing a few letters to Stella and wishing I could be there to hold my new son. I took the pictures to work the next day and made an ass of myself all over again. I sent Stella some money and promised to write every week. Having a son inspired me to work even harder. The thought of my new son sent me to a higher level. I began volunteering to work overtime.

Each day on the bus, while riding to and from work, I daydreamed about New York City. The palms of my hand would sweat and my heartbeat would quicken just thinking about that magical moment when my plane would touch down in "The Big Apple."

SNAKEBITE

I got off work late one Saturday night after doing a double shift and was hurrying to catch the midnight bus. Without thinking, I cut through an alleyway my co-workers had warned me about. They said it was infested with drug abusers. I remembered too late. Before I was halfway through the alley, I ran into a very nervous guy who asked me something in Spanish. Before I could reply, he drew a gun from his waistband and stuck it in my face. "Damalo Chawo!" I didn't know what he meant and obviously didn't move fast enough for him, so he smashed the gun into my head and repeated his demand. "Damalo Chawo, Maricon!" I staggered backwards into a brick wall, hit my head against the wall, and fell helplessly to the ground as blood began to cover my face. I could feel him cleaning out my pockets and ripping the watch off my hand, but was helpless to even try to resist, which probably was for the best.

I felt myself slipping in and out of consciousness. I just wanted to close my eyes and go to sleep, but instinctively, I knew I had to get out of there. Crawling on all fours, I made my way out of the alley and onto the sidewalk, where I passed out.

I awoke to find a bright light shining in my eyes. I wasn't asleep, but I wasn't quite awake either. I heard voices and thought I was dreaming, because two people were talking about me as if I wasn't there. A female voice said, "He's trying to open his eyes. I think he's coming to!"

My eyes were half open and I saw silhouettes of two people standing over me. I wanted to ask them what was going on and why were they shining that damn light in my face. I tried to talk, but couldn't. They were asking me stupid questions I didn't understand and my eyelids became heavy, so I slowly closed my eyes and they vanished.

I woke up with a bad headache and touched my head, which was wrapped in bandages. I didn't understand why. I looked around me. Another bed was in my room, very neatly made up with a white sheet and white pillow. This place looked like a hospital, but if it was, how did I get here and why was my head hurting so badly? Nothing made any sense.

I tried to get out of bed, but my head was hurting too badly, so I just lay there thinking, trying to remember. After a while, things started coming back slowly. My name was Conrad Bastien and I lived in Trinidad . . . I mean, I'm from Trinidad. For now, I was living at the Salvation Army in San Juan. I remembered I had a job in Rio Pierdras and that I came here on a big ship.

My memory was returning in bits and pieces, and that was scaring the living daylights out of me. It confused me and I began to wonder, what if it doesn't all come back?

Suddenly, the door to my room opened and my doctor entered. He must have seen the fear on my face, or else he was a mind reader. He said very soothingly, "Don't worry. It will all come back. It takes time, but you are going to be alright."

The doctor took a pencil light out of his pocket and examined my eyes, then held out three fingers. "How many fingers do I have up?"

I answered, "Three."

Then he asked me the year, month, country, and date. I got the date wrong because I was in and out of it for three days. When he told me about my lost days, my heartbeat quickened and the palm of my hands began to sweat.

The doctor kept me for another twenty-four hours under observation. I called my job and the Salvation Army and explained what happened. My manager and the people at the Salvation Army were very understanding and wished me a speedy recovery.

By the end of the day, it all came back to me and I felt much better. I asked my doctor what Damalo Chawo meant.

He said, "Give me the money." I wasn't very surprised.

I received very good care and after a week was released from the hospital. The pills I was given for my headache made me drowsy, but they took the pain away. I was instructed to change the bandage on my head every other day and to take my medicine as prescribed until my return visit the following week, a visit I knew I wouldn't keep.

The first thing I did upon my release was to buy a hat big enough to cover the bandage on my head. A part of me wanted to return to work and save some more money, but the flashing green light in my mind told me it was time to leave Puerto Rico.

My wallet with Kenny's baby picture, my paycheck, and $40 dollars in cash were gone. Fortunately, I kept my passport, Social Security card and my money, which I always turned into travelers' checks and kept well hidden in my room.

The folks at my job were very supportive. To my surprise, they replaced the check and the cash that were stolen. I picked up my last paycheck, thanked everyone and returned to the shelter in San Juan.

Suddenly, I felt I needed to get away from Puerto Rico in a hurry, as fast as I could, so I called a few airlines and got a cheap ticket to New York. My plane was scheduled to leave at eleven-fifteen the next morning.

I got very little sleep that night because I was much too nervous to sleep. I packed and re-packed, paced up and down, and looked out the window, searching for daylight. I checked the time every five minutes and rechecked my list of things to do once I arrived in New York.

Finally, daylight slowly began to make its appearance. That's when I remembered my flight was almost six hours away at eleven fifteen a.m. So I lay across the bed fully dressed, thinking of Stella and my new son. Eventually, I fell into a deep, dream-filled slumber. I dreamt I was at the airport and was very upset because I had just missed my flight to New York because I overslept. I became furious enough to kick myself. I was kicking something when suddenly I woke up, startled and disoriented. For a moment, I didn't know where I was or what time it was. I was in a cold sweat until I checked the time and realized I was only dreaming. It was eight ten a.m.

The thought of missing my flight really upset me, so I went out and bought my first espresso. At nine a.m., I took my bags down to the office, made a donation, thanked the officials, then went out and got a cab to the airport. Finally, I was on my way to New York.

While in the cab, I watched the city of San Juan go by. Memories of the past two years, clips of everything that happened to me on every island I had visited, from the moment I left Trinidad to the present, all came back to me one after another. I was lost in the private screening of the last two years of my life.

The cab driver had to call me a few times before I realized we were sitting at the airport. I paid him, then went in and picked up my ticket to New York.

It was only when I had my ticket that reality hit me. I was really on my way to New York. I began perspiring, my hands started shaking and I had to fight to compose myself. "I am not going to become emotional. I will not become emotional," I kept repeating to myself.

I had an enormous rush of different emotions. Until now, I had it all under control. I had been very strong. All of a sudden I was having trouble holding it together. I kept looking at the clock every few minutes and it turned out to be the longest two hours of my life.

We finally boarded and it was the biggest plane I had ever flown on. I crossed my fingers and began praying as we took off. During the flight, I thought of the struggles I had been through to get here: Of Stella and the baby. Mostly, I thought of my mom and the promises I made to her. Then I pinched myself until it hurt to make sure I wasn't dreaming.

NEW YORK AT LAST

We touched down in New York at LaGuardia Airport on a sunny Monday afternoon. Slowly, my plane began pulling up to the terminal. I dried the palms of my hands and tried to act natural. The guy sitting next to me turned and looked at me suspiciously. Maybe he heard the sound of the drums my heart was beating.

I began taking long, deep breaths in an attempt to calm myself down. Finally, the plane came to a stop and everyone prepared to exit. I followed the crowd of anxious people waiting to embrace their loved ones.

"I'm in New York," I whispered to myself. "I'm really in New York!" I picked up my luggage and took a yellow cab. Through information I had gotten from guys at the Salvation Army, I headed to Hotel St. George on Clarke St. in Brooklyn.

Looking out the window as the cab headed to Brooklyn, part of me could not believe I had made it to New York, and that was okay. Another part of me was threatening to become very emotional, and I couldn't have that. Real men don't cry, I kept reminding myself.

When we got to the hotel, I paid the cabby and was in awe at the size of the hotel. I paid for a week in advance, then took my very first elevator ride that seemed to be going up to the sky. My room was on the eighteenth floor. When I peeped out of the window, the height made me dizzy. The highest I had ever been before was on the fourth floor, and I thought that was up there.

As I put my bags down and closed the door behind me, I fell on my knees and began thanking God for bringing me safely through all those islands. For making my dreams come true. And then I pinched myself to make sure I wasn't dreaming. I knelt there reflecting briefly and wishing my mother could be here to share this sweet victory with me. I thought of Stella and the baby, and then the dam broke and I began sobbing uncontrollably. All the tears I had been holding back for so long were now running free. It was such a triumphant, victorious feeling. I had never known such sweet happiness, such euphoria. It brought so many tears of joy, because finally, I had accomplished my impossible mission.

Against all odds, I had made it. I did what everyone, except my mom, had told me I could never do and was crazy to even think of trying. At that moment, I wished I could climb to the roof of the tallest building and scream at the top of my lungs, loud enough for them to hear me all the way back in Trinidad, "I did it! I did it! I did it! I did it!"

When I calmed down a little, I thought to myself, my mother was right. With God and *The Guide* on my side, I could do anything. And so two years after leaving Trinidad at the age of sixteen with virtually no money or connections, I had accomplished the number one consuming obsession of my life, and I did it on the wings of a dream.

Now, forty years later, my children—after listening to my incredible story numerous times—convinced me to tell it. A story that magnifies the power of a dream that took wings when persistently backed by faith, persistence, desire and a strong will that did not accept defeat.

I hope my story inspires my readers to make adversity their stepping stone and pursue their dreams relentlessly until it grows wings and takes them up where they belong.

THE SIX PRINCIPLES OF THE GUIDE

In the 60's, my dream came true because it grew wings and took flight. It all began with an idea, a thought, a burning desire mixed with faith. I nourished and encouraged that burning desire until it grew into an obsession, a tidal wave that swept me away, driving me to become creative, resilient, and to find ways to do what no one believed I could.

I believe that human beings are greater, more powerful than we realize. Deep inside each and every one of us dwells a sleeping giant called Faith. When awakened, faith can drive us to move or climb any mountain. Our only limitations are the ones we impose on ourselves by acknowledging and accepting such handicaps, then allowing those mental handicaps to grow until they become disabilities.

The antidote to failure is to learn to think like an eagle. My state of mind, my burning desire, faith, willpower, discipline, persistence, my hunger; these virtues became my guiding light, my road map. Driving me forward, they brought me through the rain and storms and turned my dreams into reality. I did not let my learning disability, lack of money, education or connections to become handicaps. Instead of leaning on the crutches of excuses, I thrived on the challenge of adversity.

DESIRE

As I analyze my experience, I can certainly understand the skepticism of everyone who doubted I could do what they obviously saw as an impossible mission. To them, it seemed impossible because they saw only what I didn't have, things like experience, money, connections, and a formal education.

While they were looking at what I lacked, I was focusing on what I had, which was God and *The Guide*. And these, my friends, were all I needed for success.

Read the biography and carefully analyze the life of any successful person, from inventors and entrepreneurs to billionaires and presidents, and you will catch more than a glimpse of the role those principles played in their lives. The road to success begins with the knowledge, understanding and persistent application of these principles.

Desire is number one because that's where it all begins. A burning desire to be, to do, and to have, is the starting point from which dreams are launched. A burning desire will eventually drive you to accept nothing less than victory.

Many years ago, I was a starry eyed teenager on a tiny Caribbean Island with a burning desire to get to America and have Diana Ross sing my songs. When this desire first flashed across my mind, I was in no position to act upon it because a few difficulties stood in my way. I did not have the finances to get to America, had absolutely no connections and didn't know in which state Diana Ross lived. These difficulties did not discourage or distract me from attempting to carry out my desire, because this was no ordinary desire. It was definite. And so I decided I would island hop to America. My friends and family saw it as insanity; I saw it as a mission I had to accomplish by any means necessary.

I stood by my desire. I nurtured it with all of my energy, effort and willpower as I constantly intensified it. There was a method to my madness as I planned definite ways and means to achieve success. Then I backed those plans up with persistence, which does not recognize failure.

As fate would have it, a few years after getting to New York, I landed a job with Executive Chauffeur/Security as a chauffeur and bodyguard. They were located on 60th Street off Fifth Avenue. Little did I know at that time that Diana Ross lived only two blocks away.

A few weeks after my training, Executive Chauffeur called me into the office and informed me that they were sending me on a very important interview. It was with a celebrity who recently moved to New York City to begin filming a movie and was in need of a chauffeur/bodyguard. They didn't tell me who the celebrity was, and I did not ask.

When I got to the address of the interview, there were twenty-five other well-dressed applicants there. Listening to their gossip, I found out that the name of the celebrity was Diana Ross. I almost passed out. I also found out that she was about to begin filming *The Wiz*.

The interview began and I sat on pins and needles until my name was called. I was number thirteen. Talk about the truth being stranger than fiction. Thirteen minutes into the interview Mr. Ron, who was conducting the interview, stretched out his hand to me and, as I took it, he said the words that helped change my life forever. "Congratulations, you've got the job!" Needless to say, I was speechless.

MY BOSS DIANA ROSS

Two days later, I met my new boss, Diana Ross. When we were introduced, I took her hand and I knew exactly how stammered Ralph Cramden on "The Honeymooners" must have felt. I stood there going, "Ah ma ah ma ah ma ah ma." It was so embarrassing. Miss Ross and the others couldn't stop laughing.

Looking back on that episode of my life, I doubt it was a mere coincidence that my agency just happened to be one of the agencies Diana Ross called in search of the right chauffeur and bodyguard, and that I just happened to get lucky and beat out twenty-five other applicants. I doubt it. Many of us refuse to believe that which we do not see or really understand. However, psychologists have correctly stated that "When one is truly ready for something, it will put in its appearance."

Working for Miss Diana Ross was indeed a once in a lifetime experience. I listened very carefully and learned much from her. Of all the encouragement and advice Miss Ross gave me, one of the most important things she told me time and time again was "your dreams are the children of your soul. Never give up your dreams and never let anything or anyone stand in your way. Pursue your dreams no matter how far fetched they may seem to others. Persevere."

Talk about irony. I was so close and yet so far because I could not show Diana the songs I had written for her. I had been warned to never attempt to voluntarily discuss my personal life in any way with her. That was by far the most frustrating period of my entire life.

I was given the name of Miss Ross' recording company and was advised to submit my songs to them. I will continue to do so until she sings one of my songs or the sea stops rushing to the shore.

Diana Ross has always been and will always be a great source of inspiration to me. While in her employ, I had the pleasure of meeting some very interesting people, including Michael Jackson, Diane Von Furstenberg, Sidney Poitier, Sydney Lumet, Liza Minnelli, John Denver and Jackie Kennedy Onassis, among others.

A very enjoyable part of my job with Miss Ross was taking her three little girls, Rhonda, Tracy, and Chutney, to and from school each day. They were well-behaved and very respectful.

I also witnessed some amusing encounters between Diana Ross and her fans. While shopping in Bloomingdales, a young girl turned to Miss Ross and said, "You look exactly like Diana Ross." Miss Ross smiled and said, "You know, I hear that all the time."

We were in Woolworth, a downscale store in Manhattan, one evening when a female shopper glanced at Miss Ross dismissively and said to her girlfriend, "She looks just like Diana Ross, but she couldn't be. Diana Ross wouldn't shop in a store like this." Miss Ross and I just smiled and moved on.

When the making of *The Wiz* was complete, Miss Ross took me to her posh home in Beverly Hills, and then to her new home in Malibu. Even though I was only a hired hand, I was privileged to have spent some time getting to know some of her closet relatives, including her mother, sister, brother and husband.

A PRIVATE CONCERT

Something I will never forget about Diana Ross are the chills I would get whenever she sang a few notes while sitting in her yellow convertible Corniche Rolls Royce as I drove her around Manhattan or L.A. She had just completed her new album *The Boss*. I enjoyed working for her and sometimes I felt a little guilty when I collected my paycheck. I have reexamined the circumstances that led to my meeting Diana Ross and see it as nothing short of miraculous. It is a fact. Opportunities gravitate to those whose minds have been prepared to attract them, just as surely as a river gravitates to the ocean.

During my odyssey, there were times when I had no idea where Diana Ross lived or how I was going to meet her. But my belief was so strong that I was blind to the possibility of never meeting her. To me, it was never a question of *if*, but *when*.

So far, Diana Ross hasn't performed any of my songs, but I haven't given up hope. I believe that someday she will. Persistence is my password. It is my insurance against failure.

I cannot overstate the importance of desire because it has been the main ingredient for success in my life. Think about it. When you were a baby, desire is what made you stop crawling around, pull yourself up and, as scary as it seemed, take that first step. Back then, you desired more than anything else to learn how to walk. You sometimes cried with frustration each time you fell down. Many babies do. However, you were very determined. As many times as you fell down was as many times as you got back up and tried again. You kept at it until you mastered it. Why? Because instinctively, you believed you needed to walk. Not just wanted to, but needed to. Desire is the fire that drives your need. What you need, you find a way to get, like clothing, food, and shelter. You accept no excuses from yourself or from others. You let nothing stand in your way. If you need it, then you'll get it at any cost.

THE OBSTACLE COURSE

It isn't easy, but mama never said it would be. Everyday life itself is an obstacle course. In contrast, the road to success is filled with twice as many obstacles. It's as if the unseen forces' duty is to stop anyone who tries to enter the golden gates of success by deliberately placing stumbling blocks all along the path. These hindrances seem to stand back with grins on their faces as if to say "I dare you!" or "Do you think you are good enough to get past me?" Maybe that is why so few make it all the way to the top.

Many people find giving up or settling to be much easier than standing and fighting to the bitter end. If more people understood the power of "definite desire," and constantly nurtured this desire, they would discover it can grow into a dominating obsession that, when backed by persistence, does not recognize the word failure.

BLUEPRINT FOR SUCCESS

The following method consists of six definite steps that can help you tremendously in transmitting your burning desire into reality:

Step 1: Know exactly what you want and what you intend to give in return. Have a definite date set for that accomplishment.

Step 2: Create a clear and definite blueprint for carrying out your plans.

Step 3: Most importantly, begin today. Do not procrastinate.

Step 4: Fine tune your plan and put it in writing so it becomes tangible. Make copies and be sure to put one inside your closet door and other places you can't help but notice.

Step 5: Read your written statement aloud with faith and feeling a minimum of three times daily while visualizing every single word you say.

Step 6: Daily, make a list of the six most important things you have to do tomorrow and number them in their order of importance. Scratch off each one after completion. Put any that don't get done on the following day's list.

If you follow these instructions explicitly and truly desire to move up and succeed, then your burning desire, your obsession, will drive you to climb any mountain and overcome any obstacle you may face on your journey to success.

Never delude yourself into thinking that because you have decided to move up to a higher level, suddenly everything and everyone around you will cooperate. In fact, be prepared for just the opposite. Be ready for a battle. Take it one day, one victory at a time. Determination, focus, passion and persistence must be your passwords as you constantly intensify your desire for success.

FAITH

The second principle in *The Guide* is faith. In fact, faith, hope and love are called the theological virtues and are the most powerful of all the major emotions.

Looking back on my childhood, I can see where the love of my mother and the strength of her faith changed me from a nine-year-old child with a learning disorder into an artistic teenager who believed nothing was impossible to him. I came to understand that obstacles in my way were there to test my character and my faith. These obstacles could be used as stepping-stones on my way to victory.

As a child, I was very fortunate. My mother didn't just tell me to have faith. She taught me how. I learned that faith is a state of mind that can be developed through repeated instructions to your subconscious mind.

My mom laid it out very plain and simple for me:

1- You have the power to control your thoughts.
2- Your mind becomes magnetized by the dominating thoughts you hold within it.
3- Learn to keep out negative thoughts and emotions, such as fear, envy, greed, superstition, hate and revenge.
4- Learn to encourage and hold positive thoughts in your mind, such as love, hope, faith, romance, enthusiasm and forgiveness. (Hence the reason for such prophetic sayings as, "As a man thinketh, so he becomes; show me your friends and I'll tell you who you are; what you sow is what you'll reap," etc., etc., etc.)
5- Write out an affirmation, commit it to memory, and repeat it with faith several times daily. Consider this example: "By the first day of the first month of 2010, I will become a millionaire. I promise to work smarter and follow my master plan. I also promise to avoid bad influences and negative people like the plague. I sign my name to this affirmation and ask the Almighty for his help in keeping it."

Remember that your subconscious mind does not discriminate, nor does it differentiate. It gives the results of whatever it's been fed. Put in negative, get out negative. Put in positive, get out positive. If a person repeats a lie often and long enough, he eventually accepts that lie as the truth. We all are what we are because of the thoughts we have allowed and encouraged to flourish in the garden of our minds.

Millions of people the world over believe they have bad luck when all they really have is a bad way of thinking. Right here and now is the best time to resolve to make faith a larger part of your life.

So many people go through rituals, hoping and praying for good luck or hoping to get the right break, never thinking for a moment that it's right there in their hands, or should I say, their minds. If only they would think. If only they understood the magical power of believing.

Many years ago, it seemed impossible for a man to run a mile in under four minutes. Then in the 1950s, an English gentleman by the name of Roger Banister did it and made history. He made headlines all over the world. Not long thereafter, another athlete did the same thing. Then another, then another, then another. Why? Because they now knew and believed it could be done. The limitation that was in their minds had been removed.

Too often we hinder our own progress by placing limitations on our goals. We sometimes hear of amazing feats by ordinary people and wonder how they did it. Those who did the impossible will testify that faith can indeed move mountains.

Sounds simple, doesn't it? And it is. Why then don't more people have faith? Well, because they just don't get it. They don't understand the simplicity of the concept or the magical power of faith. Another reason more people don't get it is, because, like many of the best things in life, it's free. I believe one of the greatest weaknesses of man is his inability to truly appreciate, or value, that which is free.

WINGS OF A DREAM

Listen carefully to my new song, "Wings of a Dream." Soon, everyone everywhere will be singing it. Why? Because deep inside us all there lives a sleeping genius. A giant. We instinctively know we can fly if we really decide to put out the enormous effort it takes to do so. This beautiful song paints a picture of our true potential. It gives us a glimpse of what we can accomplish, how high we can really fly. It lifts us up high and gives us a peek into the windows of our souls, a look at our true selves. It is a musical affirmation of faith.

Just take a few minutes and listen to the beautiful words:

Verse 1

"I believe in my dream
My faith has given it wings
There are times when it seems
My dream is light years away
This feeling inside me
Is what keeps me alive
It's a hunger that drives me
And gives me the courage to stand up and say

Chorus

On the wings of a dream
With faith and persistence
Desire and a strong will
I can move any mountain
Yes I can climb every hill
Where they see a wide river
All I see is a stream
With faith as my guide I fly
On the wings of a dream

Verse 2

I will seek till I find
I'll knock until it opens
It's just a matter of time
Before the sun shines my way
A higher power is on my side
I will not be denied
Yes, my faith is the reason
I'm high on believing every word when I say

Chorus Then Fade."

This song is all about faith—the magic of believing. I conceived and believed it therefore, I can do it.

Deep inside, most people want to fly. They believe that with a little help, they can learn to fly. This is my belief. That's why I was driven to write this book. I needed desperately to share with you this wonderful gift of enlightenment and empowerment. It moves me. It saved me. It makes me want to get down on my knees and thank the Lord for this feeling that encompasses me.

Faith can do this for you. It can work miracles in your life. You do not have to live like a bird with a broken wing, is unable to fly and submits passively to the laws of its environment. You have that special something in you. With faith, you can find a way to arouse the genius that lies asleep in your brain and cause it to drive you upward to whatever goal you desire. You can charter a flight plan for success. You can reinvent yourself. Your wings are not broken; they are just tied. Following the principles outlined in this book will help you untie your wings. Flying doesn't have to be for only a chosen few. With help, you to can learn to fly.

WINNING A SCHOLARSHIP

My four years of training as an actor at the Lee Strasberg Theater Institute in New York City in the 1990s were a direct result of faith, determination, and courage. It all began in late spring of 1993. One day I walked into the lobby of my apartment building and read a notice posted on the wall. It read, "The Lee Strasberg Theater Institute will soon be holding auditions for scholarships to the school."

I couldn't believe my eyes. The very school I had researched the year before, only to discover I couldn't afford its tuition, was offering a chance to attend free of charge. Lee Strasberg is the Harvard of acting schools. It is one of the finest drama schools in the world. Its distinguished alumni include Marlon Brando, Marilyn Monroe, Al Pacino, Robert DeNiro, and many other notable performers. I literally saw the writing on the wall and was not about to let this golden opportunity slip through my fingers.

At that very moment, after reading the notice, I made up my mind that no matter what it took, I was going to win myself a scholarship. I immediately called and made arrangements to audition. That's when I learned there would be two auditions. The first was for a private agency. The second would be for Mrs. Anna Strasberg at her school the following day.

I couldn't believe my good fortune. In two days, I was going to be on stage at the acting school of my dreams, standing in the footsteps of legends. The anxiety began to bubble up inside me. I became confused. What should my audition piece be? Should I sing a song? Should I recite a poem? Should I dance or should I just get down on my knees and beg?

I changed my mind at least one hundred times. Each time I pictured myself facing the audience, my heart began doing push-ups. I finally settled on *"Face of a Stranger,"* a poem I had written and knew quite well. The night before my audition, I got very little sleep. The next day, in front of a smaller than expected audience, I passed the first audition with flying colors. But I felt something was missing. I wasn't satisfied. I didn't stand out. Other candidates also recited poems and passed. A voice kept warning me that I had to do much better tomorrow. I felt I would have to be much more imaginative if I was going to be a winner. I stayed up all night writing and memorizing a new monologue because I was determined to impress Mrs. Strasberg.

The next morning, we all met in the Marilyn Monroe Theatre of the Lee Strasberg Institute at Union Square. I was shocked by the size of the crowd. It was really standing room only. I was even more surprised when I saw the press. Cameras were everywhere as the auditions finally began. "Well, this is it!" I told myself. At first I was nervous. Then it grew. Nervous soon became terrified. I flirted briefly with the idea of leaving while I still had a chance. Then I felt like slapping myself for having such a silly thought.

My turn came and, with courage I never knew I had, I took the stage. As I looked out at the beautiful audience, I froze. For a few seconds, I couldn't find my voice. The bright lights were blinding. My hands were literally shaking, but I willed myself to perform.

COURAGE UNDER FIRE

Halfway through my monologue, I forgot my lines and drew a blank. The sound of silence was deafening. I stood there frozen, as if stuck in a time warp. Everyone was silently urging me on, but nothing came out. After what seemed like an eternity, I turned to Mrs. Anna Strasberg and said, "I'm sorry, but I really am very nervous. In fact, I'm scared to death!"

The tension broke. She and everyone else broke into laughter and cheerfully applauded my honesty. I further explained to Mrs. Strasberg and the audience that I had spent all night writing and memorizing my monologue and would really appreciate if another contestant could take my place while I regrouped. Mrs. Strasberg agreed.

I later returned to the stage a little more relaxed. Not only did I get through it, but I also received a standing ovation. It had me almost in tears.

After a short intermission, the performers returned to the auditorium. Mrs. Strasberg took the stage and began reading the results. Many names were called and the winners applauded. She was now very close to the end of the list and I was sweating bullets. Finally she said, "And the last scholarship goes to Mr. Conrad Bastien!" I almost passed out. I was having trouble breathing and couldn't answer her when she called my name. She had to call it twice. Everyone was hysterical as they watched me holding my chest and looking as if I were about to have a coronary.

I later learned that Mrs. Strasberg liked my monologue, which was about the attempted abuse of my teenage daughter by her ex-boyfriend. Even more importantly, she liked my direct and simple honesty under pressure.

FACING YOUR FEARS

Something that could have been a bad break, forgetting my lines, instead turned out to be the very reason I won the scholarship. Courage played the biggest part of that day. Of course I was terrified, but I knew I had to do anything necessary to succeed. So I faced my fear head on and with confidence.

It's alright to be afraid. Just don't let fear paralyze or control you. Make it a stepping-stone to victory. On the winding road to success, you are going to have a few challenging situations. This is to be expected. Mama never said it was going to be a piece of cake. Ask any soldier, firefighter, or police officer and they will tell you there have been times that they too have been scared in the face of danger. But when the blood pumps and the adrenaline flows, courage comes into play and instinct takes over to put fear on the run. These heroes find the courage to do whatever must be done.

A hero is not a man of steel who is never afraid. A hero is one who summons the courage to be brave in the face of danger and does whatever is necessary without hesitation. Heroes are people who accomplish great things under difficult circumstances by putting their hopes above their fears.

If you analyze Sylvester Stallone's character in any one of his *Rocky* films, you will see the meaning of the word courage. These movies may help you understand that there is a silent and irresistible power that comes to the rescue of the fighter who doesn't know how to quit, one who is blind to the possibility of defeat.

The four years I spent at the Lee Strasberg Theater Institute were four of the most wonderful years of my life. I learned so much more than play-writing and the method of acting. I got a priceless education because I learned the importance of faith in a world of make believe.

I had a full scholarship, so I had to attend quite a few classes each day. Needless to say, studying all day and working every evening was very challenging, but I enjoyed school and was determined to succeed.

I will always be grateful to Mrs. Anna Strasberg for helping me become a playwright and an actor. Even more importantly, I am thankful to her for giving me wings. She believed in me and enlightened me. Learning was easy because I was surrounded by love.

THE ACTING BUG

The months flew by, and as the first year ended, not only was I getting "Acting Fever," I lived in a constant state of excitement. I discovered it to be a different world. My nervousness quietly became excitement because the work was fun. I enjoyed every aspect of it. Acting became a sincere passion, and I had unmatched enthusiasm for my craft.

My second and third years at Strasberg passed as a blur. During my fourth and final year, I got a call late one evening from Miss Elizabeth Kemp, one of my instructors, and herself an excellent actress. She was in rehearsals for a play, Gorky's *The Lower Depths* at The Actors' Studio. Miss Kemp wanted me to audition for a part made available because someone had just been fired. I got to the Actors' Studio in record time, auditioned and got the part. During my introduction to the cast, I was surprised and elated to meet the star of the play, Oscar winner Tatum O'Neal. She and the rest of the cast were very supportive.

This was my first big play, but I was ready. For the next seven weeks, I got very little sleep. There were classes from nine to five, followed by rehearsals from six until sometimes two in the morning.

Finally, the play opened and was a huge success. I was walking on air! Not only was I in a hit play at The Actors' Studio with my favorite teacher, but I was also working with the youngest Academy Award winner ever. Dreams really do come true.

Other plays and small roles in low-budget films followed, but none were as thrilling as working with Tatum O'Neal. She had a great personality and her enthusiasm was infectious. Even now, I can still hear her saying to me, "Success is right there for the taking, but you have to want it more than anything else. Remember Conrad, there is always room at the top."

TO HER WITH LOVE

As my fourth year ended at the Institute, I wanted to honor Mrs. Anna Strasberg so she would know just how much I appreciated what she had done for me. I wrote and recorded this demo song for her. It's appropriately entitled "To Her With Love".

"TO HER WITH LOVE"
WORDS AND MUSIC BY CONRAD BASTIEN

Verse 1

I wrote this song to tell the world
About a very special girl.
When I was down she came to me
And showed how great a love can be.
She gave my life a new beginning
She helped me leave my past behind.
Made me believe I am a diamond
And then she taught me how to shine!

Chorus

To her with love,
These simple words are all that I can say,
But they only begin to tell the way.
I truly feel inside, thank God she's on my side.
Since I can't give her the very moon and
Stars that shine above,
I dedicate this song to her, to her with love.

Verse 2

How can I help but sing about her?
She is the reason I survive.
She gave me hope, she gave me courage,
Till I was strong enough to fly.
Now I can face the world again,
Her love has turned my life around,
But in my heart I know, without her,
I'd still be in the lost and found.

Chorus

To her with love,
These simple words are all that I can say,
But they only begin to tell the way,
I truly feel inside, thank God she's on my side.
Since I can't give her the very moon an
Stars that shine above,
I dedicate this song to her, to her with love.
Repeat Chorus then fade

WILLPOWER

The third principle in *The Guide* is willpower, one of the most important principles in this guide to success. It is the key, the oasis in the desert of lost hope, for which many of us have been searching.

We all know right from wrong, and most of us know exactly what we need to do to become successful. However, research has shown time and again that some of the easiest things to comprehend are often the most difficult to do.

As you read these lines today, at this very moment, there are people who are ready. They are standing tall, going deep within themselves, and finding the strength, willpower and determination to take full control of their lives to become successful.

Willpower is this powerful because it is a magical combination of desire, determination, discipline, drive, faith, and perseverance.

This unbeatable combination of principles makes willpower the supreme ruler of the mind. In fact, it is the President or Chairman of the mind. It surpasses all else in power or preeminence because it has the final say in all our decisions. Willpower has the ability to carry out one's wishes or plans regardless of opposition or outside influences.

A handful of people the world over seem to possess a supernatural will. Many others have a strong will. Then there are those with average wills and weak wills. A strong will can change the ordinary into extraordinary. It can be the difference between an also-ran and being the winner.

SALESMAN OF THE YEAR

When I moved to Rocky Mount, North Carolina, and began selling cars in mid-2004, I was new to the area and the business of sales. Some of my co-workers had been selling cars for seven, ten, fifteen and twenty years and had developed large customer bases. Even though I was new at this, I was a veteran to the business of desire, faith, willpower, and other principles of success. In my corner were three of the best teachers in this business: Jay Hooks, Stephen Dollar, and Kevin Benton. They trained me and believed in me, and my confidence soared.

My second month at Alliance Suzuki, I won the Salesman of the Month Award and never looked back. Nineteen months later, I won the Salesman of the Year Award.

We can't all have a supernatural will like Michael Jordan, but with concentration of effort, we all can develop and strengthen our power of will. We can begin by taking baby steps and working our way up to bigger things. Use it or lose it. There are many things you need to do that you put off for another time. Well, starting with the smallest one, tackle that task today. For instance, start exercising even for as little as five minutes daily. Or resist the temptation and smoke one or two fewer cigarettes. Or take a smaller helping of food and leave a little more on your plate. How about making the phone calls you've been putting off? Or walking two or three blocks a day, then adding on a few as you begin to feel stronger?

I believe that you know the areas of your life where you can start to exercise your willpower. As you master these little things, you can begin to give yourself bigger challenges. Keep in mind that you will also be strengthening your discipline. And as a bonus, you will slowly begin to eliminate two of your most dangerous handicaps procrastination and complacency.

My children and grandchildren sometimes ask me to lighten up because I often stress the importance of understanding and living by *The Guide*. However, each time I tell them about my country and the conditions of my childhood, they seem amazed. My family would like to visit my country someday, but they definitely wouldn't care to live there. In fact, they said they cannot begin to understand surviving some of the conditions I grew up around, such as walking a few miles to and from the river whenever it didn't rain for a few weeks, having no electricity or indoor plumbing, or walking a few miles each day to and from school. And these were just the small inconveniences. After hearing about the way life was for me when I was a child, they sometimes seem a little more understanding of my great desire for them to finish school and become successful.

I truly believe that if all Americans, during their early teenage years, had to live for a minimum of six months with a poor family in a third world country, they would inevitably acquire a much greater appreciation for the unlimited opportunities many of them take for granted. They would also understand why millions of people from every country on the planet are risking their lives day after day to reach this *Promised Land.* America.

Some of these foreigners who go through hell to get here may not have had much schooling academically, but are well schooled in the principles of success.

To get to America, they were fueled by desire, determination, faith, courage, discipline, control, willpower, and an I-will-not-be-denied attitude. Some of them grew up in their countries with very little except hope and a dream in their hearts, these principles were ingrained in them from their early childhood. They became a way of life, a way of survival. They are driven; failure is not an option.

That leads me to believe that if by some kind of miracle I could find a way to market *The Guide*, I would put it into bottles. Then I would send a bottle of these life-changing principles, free of charge, to every one of my readers. I would do this because it is my dearest hope that everyone who reads this book will become inspired, motivated, and determined to make his or her dreams come true. Make no mistake about it, dreams do come true. My ex-boss, Diana Ross, once told me, "No matter how outrageous or absurd your dream may seem to others, if you believe in it, you should hold onto it and not let anyone kill it or take it away from you." She was right.

TWENTY-FIVE YEARS OF HOPING

Let me share with you a very personal miracle that I believe was the direct result of holding onto a dream. In the mid 1990s, while I was still attending the Lee Strasberg Theater Institute, the son I had not seen in twenty-five years found me. When he was three-months-old, his mother took him and vanished into thin air. I came home from work and they were gone. The apartment was as empty as the day we first moved in.

I searched everywhere and contacted everyone I knew, but to no avail. It was as if they had disappeared. As the years went by, I continued to check the schools. I went back to St. Luke Hospital at 114th and Amsterdam Avenue in Manhattan, where Conrad Bastien Jr. was born, and obtained a copy of his birth records. With these records in hand, I kept checking the school system, but got nowhere. I also never gave up hope. Even after I got married and had more kids, I never stopped hoping that one day I would see my son again.

The years passed and I often wondered where my son was, what he looked like, and what kind of man he had become. Then one day twenty-five years later, private detectives came knocking at my door. I thought I was in trouble with the law until they asked me if I had a son named Conrad Bastien, Jr.

I said yes and explained the story to them. That's when they told me that my son, through his agent and attorneys, had been searching for me for the past five years. I was speechless. My son, now twenty-five years old, was a professional basketball player in Italy at the time. The detectives immediately contacted him by phone and handed it to me. I heard the sound of his voice and tears of joy that I had been holding back so well for the past few minutes began to flow. This was the moment I had dreamed of for a quarter of a century.

One week later, my son and I were reunited. There are no words to describe how I felt that day, but it is a day I will never forget. When we met, I just hugged him for a long time and tried not to become too emotional.

We enjoyed a two-hour lunch. The reason I could not find my son for all those years was because his mother remarried and her new husband adopted him, so his last name became McRae.

Conrad Jr. attended and played basketball for Syracuse University from 1989 to 1993. Washington took him in the second round of the 1991 NBA draft. Then he was cut from the team and went to play in the Italian A-1 League with the Pallacaniesto Triests. He could even speak several languages.

One of the first questions I asked my son was if his mother had told him the truth about me and the reason I was not a part of his life. He told me that she had. This was very important to me because I did not want him to think I deserted him and his mother.

After lunch, I took Conrad back to my school to meet some of my friends and colleagues. The girls went crazy over him. From that day forward, I had lunch or dinner with my son whenever his busy schedule permitted.

TOMORROW NEVER CAME

Just as Conrad Jr. and I were getting to know each other, I received a phone call late one night. My son had collapsed and died on the basketball court at the University of California-Irvine on his first day of practice with the Orlando Magic basketball team. Apparently, he suffered from an irregular heartbeat.

After twenty-five years of hoping and dreaming I had found my son, only to have him taken away from me in the prime of his life. Only a parent who has lost a child can know what I went through.

A year after Conrad's death, as a part of my healing process, I was able to write the following song, which will be recorded one way or another. This song will help to keep his memory alive:

"THE OTHER WAY AROUND"

It seems like only yesterday
You were born
The years flew by
I blinked my eyes
And just like that, you're gone
Now memories are all I have to cling to
Your baby pictures I hold close and sing to

Chorus

What might have been
Will never be my son
At twenty-nine
Conrad, you were so young.
It breaks my heart
To have to sing this song
'Cause it should have been
The other way around.

Verse 2

Maybe there was something more
I could have done
Sometimes it seems
Like a bad dream
That I can't wake up from
But only God knows why
You went away
You're with Him now
I know we'll meet again one sweet day

Chorus

What might have been
Will never be my son
At twenty-nine
Conrad, you were so young.
It breaks my heart
To have to sing this song
'Cause it should have been
The other way around

Bridge

I'd trade places in a minute if I could
My life I would give
So you could live
Your life had only just begun

Repeat Chorus

    As I look back on the life and death of my son, I thank God for bringing him back into my life for two wonderful years before taking him away for good. At first, I was very angry. I couldn't understand how such a thing could happen. Parents are not supposed to bury their children. It's supposed to be the other way around.

    Slowly, as time went by, God gave me the strength to accept what had happened and not question His judgment. I learned it was not my place to do so. And instead of complaining, I thanked God for bringing my son back into my life.

    After a quarter of a century, my dreams, hope and faith were rewarded. For that, I give thanks to the Almighty. For a long time after the death of my son, I analyzed and re-analyzed my life. Searching, trying to find out what I could have done differently that could have saved my son's life. I read and then I reread the report that said he suffered from an irregular heartbeat, and yet I couldn't stop blaming myself. Even now, I often wonder if there was something more I could have done.

    Who knows why things happen the way they do? Once upon a time, I thought I had all the answers, but now I know all I have are questions.

    Life is truly a beautiful thing, a very precious gift. So live each day like it is your last. Don't procrastinate. Really look at those closest to you and make an effort to spend more time with them. Try to be more open, understanding, and forgiving. Look at the people you love and say from your heart, "I love you. I honestly do." Then give them each a great big hug. Don't wait for sickness, disaster or death to bring your family together. Be the catalyst, the strong one. Pick up the phone, write a letter, send smoke signals—whatever. Get the family together, especially those distant folks who feel like they are outsiders. Take the initiative and make the call today.

    They say the best things in life are free, but it was only after I learned to take time out to appreciate the little things in this beautiful world that I began to really understand that philosophy. Exercising your willpower each day by trying a little harder to do a little better than you did yesterday will bring you closer to your goal.

CHANGE IS INEVITABLE, GROWTH IS OPTIONAL

To expect change and progress in your life without first changing some things you do daily is to delude yourself. The habits you formed, whether you believe it or not, are now forming you. As each day goes by, you are in the process of becoming better or worse, depending on how you think and what you do daily.

Because of your free will, an irrevocable gift given to you by The Almighty, you can choose to be strong, think positively, and grow as you form habits of success. Or you can be weak, think negatively, and subsequently form habits of failure. One thing is certain, and that is change. Your life is changing daily for better or for worse, depending on what you give to yourself. Motivating yourself and striving for constant improvement will surely get you to the next level, but this takes willpower and discipline. Always remember this: the potential that exists within you is limitless. You've got the power. It's all in your hands.

DISCIPLINE

Discipline is the fourth principle in *The Guide* to success. The importance of this principle in our lives is so often taken for granted that, in some cases, the lack of it becomes a gigantic pitfall. Without discipline, attempting to reach your goal would be like playing the lottery. You could get very lucky and hit it, but your chances are one in a million.

Take a good look around at some of the successful people you know. Then examine the lives of a few of the unsuccessful people you know and you will see the major role that discipline, or the lack of it, has played.

Some people say that knowledge is power. I say knowledge is *potential* power. It's not what you know, but what you do with that knowledge that matters. Without discipline, it is extremely difficult to do the right thing, even if you know what the right thing is.

Education will not replace discipline. After all, educated derelicts are not uncommon. Genius will not replace discipline; disregarded genius can be found in every state. Talent will not replace it either. From New York to Los Angeles, there are many talented but undisciplined actors and entertainers who will never enter the gates of success.

Discipline and willpower equal success. It is a divine blessing to know that discipline, willpower, faith or desire can be cultivated. It all comes back to desire. You have to want, need and have a strong desire to become successful. In other words, you must be ready.

My dear mother said it best: "You can take a horse to the river, but you can't make him drink until he's ready."

I'm keeping my fingers crossed that most of the readers of this book are ready to take these lessons and run with them, share them with others and help them to become ready. In turn, they will pass it on and on until it becomes an awesome chain of inspiration, a captivating, enlightening and empowering subject shared by folks all over the world.

The same method I described in the previous chapter for developing your willpower can be used for developing your discipline. If you are ready, you will find the method to be quite simple. Keep in mind at all times that you are in control of your own progress, or lack of it, because your growth is regulated by your controlling desire. This gives you the opportunity to become as good as your most dominant aspiration.

In the early sixties, I left my country as a very determined young man with virtually no money. I had a dream in my heart. Two years later, I had island hopped my way to New York. I went through Hell to get there, but I made it. How? I had a strong desire, a definite plan, faith, determination and every other principle mentioned in this book. I believed then as strongly as I believe now that I am the master of my fate and the captain of my soul. In fact, I believe we are all masters of our fate.

When I first got the true meaning of this philosophy, I felt as though a little silent bomb of revelation burst inside me. It was so enlightening. I felt empowered, invigorated.

CHOICES, NOT EXCUSES

Choices. It is such a simple word, yet volumes can be written on its importance. When facing a dilemma, you can choose to do the wrong thing, do nothing, take the easy way out, then settle and make excuses. Or you can choose to think, be courageous, look at The Big Picture and be strong. Winners survive and thrive because they choose to see adversity for what it really is . . . . a stepping stone.

Life is about choices. Some of us waste precious time and energy casting blame and making excuses to justify failure, but the cold hard truth is the choices we have made along the way have placed us in the position we are today. The good news is that today we can choose to make a firm commitment to ourselves to summon the willpower and find the courage to make smarter choices.

God has also blessed you with the power of will. He gave you a free will. He created us all in his image. Everything you need to help better your position in life is right there inside you. Unlike the animals, you are governed by much more than just instinct. You have the God-given power to make choices and a free will to help you climb any mountain you choose. You are therefore the master of your fate because you have the power to control your thoughts and subsequently your actions. You are the captain of your soul because you have a will to do your bidding.

You can choose to invoke your willpower and self-control to become disciplined. In fact, you can stand up and say it loud: "I AM THE MASTER OF MY FATE!" That's right. Shout it out: "I AM THE MASTER OF MY FATE!" Say it again! "I AM THE MASTER OF MY FATE!" Very good! Don't you ever forget that!

Excuses are like viruses, but much worse. If you have them, you should get rid of them. The sooner, the better. As you pursue success in whatever field you choose, the powers that be will not accommodate, compensate for or tolerate excuses. Instead of making excuses, it would sometimes be much wiser to say, "I'm sorry. It's my fault. I accept full responsibility and I assure you it won't happen again." Or "I am not sure I have the right answer, but I will find out for you right away."

Some people are hooked on making excuses. They have what they believe to be clever excuses for failure. But as justifiable as some excuses are, they can never be used for money. The world wants to know one thing and one thing only: Are you successful? The world is not interested in why you almost but didn't win, no matter how wonderful your excuse may be.

SELF-ANALYSIS

I believe most of us expect a lot from life, so we should demand much more from ourselves. *Know thyself* is the oldest of all admonitions. It is imperative you get to know yourself inside and out. To help you examine yourself very carefully, I have compiled an invaluable self-analysis test. Get very well acquainted with your strengths and your weaknesses. Find the courage to do an honest analysis of your faults as you would with any real-life enemy, and try to see yourself as you really are. Then locate and eliminate these subtle, but very dangerous, enemies.

It would do you a world of good to have someone check your answers, someone who will not permit you to delude yourself.

1. Do I understand the importance of having a positive mental attitude? Do I encourage positive emotions, such as Love, Faith, Romance, Desire, and Enthusiasm, while I deliberately block out negative influences and keep my mind busy with positive thoughts?
2. Do I avoid negative emotions at all costs? Can I ignore emotions like Fear, Greed, Deceit, Hate, Envy, and Revenge?
3. Have I been working diligently towards my established goals?
4. Are my plans organized and placed in writing so I can analyze or revise them?
5. Do I pray enough, seeking wisdom and knowledge?
6. What is my major purpose in life? Why am I here?
7. Do I try to create my own breaks, or do I sit and hope to get lucky?

8. Am I guilty of procrastination or complacency?
9. Am I guilty of talking too much and listening too little?
10. Can I tell the difference between real friends and snakes in the grass?
11. Do I keep my own council?
12. Do I allow other people to do my thinking for me?
13. Am I attracted to the company of eagles or chickens?
14. Do I have a pleasing or repelling personality?
15. Am I guilty of caring too much about what other people say about me?
16. Do I learn from my mistakes?
17. When I am upset, do I rely on liquor, drugs or cigarettes to calm my nerves?
18. Am I always seeing faults in others but rarely, if ever, in myself?
19. Do I eat right, and get enough sleep, exercise and recreation?
20. Do I often feel the need to be around friends and have their approval?
21. Do I always try to be imaginative?
22. Am I guilty of believing only that which I can see and touch?
23. Am I guilty of indecision and indifference?
24. Do I put God first in everything I do?
25. Do I avoid negative people and shield my mind against all negative influences?
26. Do I indulge, secretly or openly, in gambling, drinking, or other bad habits?
27. Do I spend too much time and money on the opposite sex?
28. Am I overly aggressive or too passive?
29. Am I confident and assertive?
30. Are my priorities in order? Do I check and recheck them occasionally?

Being impartial will not be easy. That is why it is strongly suggested you enlist the aid of someone who knows you well, someone who won't just tell you what you want to hear. For the next few weeks, you should study the questions and your answers very carefully. Find out what is wrong with you and begin correcting it. As you do, you will begin to grow.

You can be your own therapist. After all, who knows you better than you know yourself? You are now in possession of all the building materials. The question you must now ask yourself is, "How badly do I want to learn to fly?"

PERSEVERANCE

Perseverance is the fifth principle in my guide to success. With the help of perseverance, by the time I was eighteen I had island hopped my way through the West Indies to America. Like millions of foreigners before me, I dreamt of a better life and pursued it relentlessly. And even though my journey here seemed like an impossible mission I was one of the lucky ones.

You may or may not be aware of it, but many people have lost their lives attempting to get to the *Promised Land*. America. I was very fortunate to survive my treacherous ordeal, get to America, get married, have children and now ten grandchildren.

Sometimes I look back on my great adventure, the risks I took and the danger I faced, and it does seem a little off the wall. Back then, it seemed quite natural to me.

The family and friends I left behind said it was insane. In retrospect, maybe they were right. In those days, it was either follow my dream regardless of the cost or remain in Trinidad to live in poverty and die slowly.

It is very easy for anyone who isn't me to say I could have stayed there, worked and saved up the plane fare, but that would have taken me years. Besides, no one could see the hunger that was driving me. The unquenchable inferno blazing through the walls of my imagination, lighting up the pictures I wanted to see as it burned away the impossibilities. A transformation occurs when a dream grows wings and take flight, when a burning desire becomes a consuming obsession.

Perseverance and other principles of *The Guide* are what got me to America, not money. My desire to get to the U.S. and become a rich and famous singer/songwriter grew into an obsession. It drove me to invent ways to accomplish my mission. I no longer recognized words like *can't* or *impossible*. I was driven, determined, motivated, focused, and passionate about my objective, and I was prepared to persevere to the end.

Because of the teachings of my mother from an early age, these principles became my way of thinking. I had nothing else going for me except God and *The Guide*. So I listened, I believed, and I learned. When push came to shove, I had the fortitude, the courage and faith to go against all odds and to pursue the dream I believed in.

At sixteen, it was easy to be dazzled by the possibilities and blinded to the danger or impossibilities. I think it is a giddy feeling few have experienced. It is the magic of risking everything for a dream nobody sees but you.

Many years ago, a man by the name of Henry Ford, who I understand never finished high school yet was driven by a dream and a burning desire to succeed, constantly educated himself and eventually proved to the world how amazing the awesome power of perseverance can be. During the early stages of producing the V-8 engine, Mr. Ford followed a dream he alone could see, which was building an engine with eight cylinders cast in one block. Everyone around him told him it couldn't be done, but he thought differently. He went against his highly-educated engineers and advisors by insisting they remain on the job until they found a way to build it.

Mr. Ford knew that doing the impossible took a little longer, so keeping his mind tightly closed against negative influences, he instructed his workers to keep at it until they found a way to produce the V-8 motor. Some of his workers obviously thought he had lost his mind as weeks turned into months with no sign of success in sight. Time went by and the engineers kept trying. Then one day, as if by a stroke of magic, success! They got it. Because of their perseverance, they found a way to do the impossible. Actually, because of Mr. Ford's perseverance he found a way to do the impossible. Had it been up to his engineers, the V-8 motor may never have been invented. Mr. Ford clearly understood the awesome power of perseverance. He also seemed to understand that he was the master of his fate.

Some said Ford got lucky. Nonsense! I think he created his own favorable break by displaying unwavering persistence and standing by his decision to produce, one way or another, the V-8 engine. He also did this by refusing to compromise his convictions, even when it meant going against his engineers, many of whom had more schooling and college degrees than he did.

In any undertaking, perseverance is one of the most important principles of success. In fact, pursuing success without perseverance would be like attempting to make steel without carbon.

EDUCATION

There were many who underestimated Mr. Ford. They made the mistake of assuming that because he did not get very far in school, he was not an educated man. Obviously, they did not understand the true meaning of the word education. An educated man is one who has developed the faculties of his mind to the point where he clearly understands the principles of success and applies them persistently towards the achievement of his objective. Henry Ford was such a man.

Don't get me wrong. Pursuing a college degree is much more than just a worthwhile endeavor. Without the principles of success to go with it, however, any degree would have serious limitations.

I do not have an innate prejudice against formal schooling. In fact, like every other parent, I believe our children's educations are of paramount importance and have to be at the very top of our list of priorities. I also believe the principles of success and financial education belong at the top of that list as well. My aim here is to give hope and encouragement to all those who have ambition and dream of success, but lack a formal education.

Some people go through life with an inferiority complex because they never finished school. Well, I must inform them that Thomas Edison and Henry Ford are two of the many great success stories who, without much formal schooling, wrote their names deep into the history books and the memories of generations to come. To assume that degrees or high IQ scores automatically equal success can be an expensive error in judgment.

Success is not always linked to college degrees. In the world outside of academics, something more than good grades is required. That extra something is what will make all the difference in your life.

I find it absolutely astounding that Thomas Edison, the godfather of perseverance, had very little schooling. However, because of his perseverance, Mr. Edison became one of the world's greatest inventors, holding more patents than any other human being dead or alive. *Life Magazine* named him the Man of the Millennium. All this for a man who persevered through over 10,000 failed attempts to find the right material for the incandescent light bulb. Through the course of his lifetime, Edison demonstrated the importance of perseverance to the world.

Many people credit Edison's ability to learn as a creative genius. I believe he credited it to persistence and hard work. Edison was an optimist who chose to view his thousands of setbacks not as failures, but as steps that brought him closer to a solution that he never doubted he would find.

At the first sign of defeat, some are quick to give up. I daresay that lack of perseverance is a major cause of failure in too many lives. What's sad is that the majority of people who gave up too soon will never know how close they came to success.

Sometimes, defeat deliberately shows up and hangs around long enough to obscure your view of victory. That is why perseverance, even in the face of defeat, is very crucial to success. Fortunately, perseverance is a state of mind that can be developed.

Remember that the starting point of all achievement is desire. Weak desires bring weak results. The intensity of your desire will decide how easy, or how difficult, cultivating the state of mind known as *persistence* will be for you. Here are some pointers that will help you train yourself to become more persistent:

1. Know exactly what you want and be determined to fight to the bitter end to get it.
2. A burning desire that drives and motivates you to go the extra mile.
3. Definite plans, in writing, frequently analyzed and repeated faithfully on a daily basis.
4. Researching, understanding, and really liking what you do.
5. Focusing on your objective as if your entire future depended on its success.
6. A mind closed against all negative influences.
7. A strong conviction that cannot be compromised by anyone or anything.
8. Not beating up yourself if you fall, but picking yourself up and becoming even more determined to succeed.
9. Having supreme faith in God and yourself and being prepared for the long haul.
10. Perseverance and concentration of effort can take you there.

I've often looked back on the major role a lack of perseverance played in the breakup of my marriage and subsequent divorce many years ago. I was blessed the day I found shy and reclusive seventeen-year-old Cathy La'Verne Glenn. I knew she was the one. I was new to America and she was everything I dreamt about and more. I courted her persistently and wooed her until I won her. She was a most beautiful bride. Our wedding day was the happiest day of our lives.

The years rolled by, kids came along and somewhere along the way, like a fool, I stopped doing all the wonderful things I did to get her. Too late, I learned that getting a good thing and keeping a good thing are as different as a liability is from an asset.

NEVER-ENDING HONEYMOON

Now, many years later, I am a bachelor who dates occasionally and may get married again someday if and when I find "Mrs. Right." Most of my buddies are married and I often listen very attentively as they complain to me about their marital problems. However, after asking them a few simple "when was the last time you . . ." questions and getting their very predictable answers, I often end up telling them what they don't want to hear. "Stop acting like a 'husband' and go back to acting like when you first met her. Become her 'boyfriend' again. Be her 'lover,' her fiancé." I remind them that the same methods they used to get their wives they must now be expanded to keep the love new and exciting. I encourage them to think, to use their imagination.

I enjoy playing coach because I get a lot of satisfaction when I help to reignite a marriage. Besides, I could become a husband again someday. I am not looking, but I don't rule it out. If it does happen, it will be very special. Very different. Where is it written that the honeymoon has to end?

I do believe that the next time I fall in love and get married, it will last forever. Month after month, year after year, I will never stop surprising her with flowers, gifts, love letters, vacations, candlelight dinners, trips to see the sunset and sunrise, bubble baths, and massages, and reminding her how wonderful she is and how lucky I am to have her in my life. In other words, I will dedicate my life to keeping my happy marriage a never-ending honeymoon.

LITTLE THINGS MEAN A LOT

Time and again, I've heard men say, "If I made more money, I would be able to do more for my lady and make her happier."

To these men I say, "Little things mean a lot." Here is an example. Many years ago, because of some bad choices I made, my life became a nightmare. Everything that could go wrong went wrong, and then some. I lived in Hell for what seemed like an eternity as I fought an uphill battle to get myself back on track.

Then miraculously, I met an angel named Dorothy Rose. Heaven only knows what she saw in me. Slowly we got to know each other and became friends. She became by bridge over troubled waters and, to her, I will always be grateful. Because of Dorothy, I survived and eventually thrived.

Two years later, while reminiscing with tears in her eyes, Dorothy showed me a roll of Life Savers and said, "I appreciate every one of your gifts, but the most precious gift you've given me is not the diamonds or the pearls. It is this roll of Life Savers. As you hugged me and called me your 'true life saver,' this is one roll of Life Savers that will never be opened."

Here are fifty little things that will mean a lot to your lady. Fifty things any man can do for his lady without spending any cash:

1. Serve her breakfast in bed.
2. Take her to see the sunset or sunrise.
3. Spend quality time with her.
4. Sing to her even if you sound like a toad.
5. Open the door for her.
6. Hold her hand as you walk slowly in the rain.
7. Practice really listening to her.
8. Touch her hair when you pass her chair.
9. Encourage and inspire her to dream big.
10. Hug and squeeze her every day.
11. Hold her chair as she sits or rises.
12. Call her up just to tell her how you feel about her.
13. Fix her a romantic, candle-lit bubble bath with soft relaxing music.
14. Slowly lotion her body, starting with her toes.
15. Hold her close as you dance slowly in the dark . . . . slowly.
16. Help her dress . . . or undress.
17. Encourage her to tell you how her day was.
18. Take time to really get to know her.
19. Send her love letters and cards.
20. Pick her a bunch of wildflowers.
21. Remind her how good she looks, how special she is and how lucky you are to have her in your life.
22. Watch her as she sleeps.
23. Kiss her good morning and love her like the devil when you get back home.
24. Take her for a moonlit walk.
25. Show her a bright star, one you'll both remember, and name it after her.
26. Have a pillow fight and create your own ending. Use your imagination.

27. Pack a basket and take her on a picnic wherever.
28. Bend to one knee, then untie and retie her shoelace.
29. Compliment everything she does.
30. Give her a pedicure, then foot massage.
31. Tell her old flames can't hold a candle to her.
32. Remind her how much you need her.
33. Thank her parents for raising such a wonderful young lady.
34. Find out what makes her happy.
35. Read poetry to her and let her know how she inspires you.
36. Take her on a slow walk down a quiet country road.
37. Give her a slow, sensuous massage.
38. Take her to the lake and feed the ducks.
39. Hold her hand at home and in public.
40. Put her picture on your t-shirt.
41. Make every day Valentine's Day.
42. Leave a trail of love notes where she'll find them.
43. Camp out in the living room with her.
44. Be totally unselfish with her.
45. Call radio stations and dedicate a love song to her.
46. Occasionally, thank God aloud for sending her into your life.
47. Share a new hobby with her.
48. Find the right pet name for her.
49. Find out her favorite everything.
50. Put drops of honey on her fingers then slowly remove it . . . . creatively.

Think hard and I'm certain you will add some wonderfully exciting things to this list. So, regardless of your financial status, the power to make your lady happier is now in your possession. Whatever you do, be sure to spend quality time with her. Be imaginative and give her the greatest gift of all: love.

In my past as well as yours, there are things we would like to alter. The reality of it is that you can't change the past. Whatever has happened in your life, both good and bad, cannot be altered.

The good news is that because of your will and your freedom of choice, you can direct and arrange your future and make it whatever you want it to be. With God and *The Guide* on your side, you can accomplish just about anything.

Perseverance can be the key. I've been pursuing my singing and songwriting career for over forty years. Still I am always writing and recording new songs and am convinced, now more than ever, that I will soon get that lucky break that has been eluding me for decades. The rest will be history. I believe my songs are that good. Some of them will become classics someday. My perseverance will soon payoff big time. I'm sure of it.

PRIDE AND DIGNITY

Pride and dignity are last on the list of principles my mother called *The Guide*. Yet in everything she taught me, they came first. The essence of her teaching was to understand and believe that nothing is impossible. Nothing can hold you back if you are ready, not even a lack of money, education or connections. An indomitable spirit will always find a way. My hope is that everyone who reads my book will say, "If a teenager from a tiny Caribbean island can take *The Guide* and learn to fly, I'm sure I can."

Adversity does reveal man to himself. This is not just a philosophical statement in a chapter; it is a very important fact of life taking place in many people's lives at this very moment.

I know of a close, unambitious relative who never seems to worry about food, shelter or bills. He has fantastic excuses why he is not working and is not seriously job-hunting. This same relative makes one bad choice after the other and never stops complaining about bad breaks and how hard life is for him. On the flip side of this type of person are the people all over the world with none of the modern, everyday conveniences we take for granted, and who are on this very day are making great sacrifices to get to America. Within two weeks of getting here, some of them will be working. A few short years later, some will be in better financial positions than others who were born and raised here. Why do you think that is?

It comes back to the principles of success. Anyone who is ready and is driven by faith, desire, willpower, determination and other principles of success can make their dreams come true.

Becoming successful in America is an exciting challenge that millions of foreigners from dozens of countries seem to live for. Let's stop and think for a moment. Why is it that people from every country on the face of the earth pour into this great nation every day? People are literally dying to get to America. They sneak onto ships, boats, trucks, cars and planes onto anything that is moving in the direction of America. Some pay a king's ransom, while others pay with their lives. The Border Patrol is overworked because people attempt to enter this country every hour of every day. Why? Because this is the greatest country on the planet.

Foreigners say that the streets of America are paved with gold. And they are, because there are golden opportunities everywhere. If you are ready to make the sacrifices necessary to realize your dreams, now is the best time for you to stake your claim and go to work.

In this book, you'll find the tools you're going to need. In your search for gold, the philosophy of this book can serve as the needed machinery. It can help you discover the shining ore and bring it to the surface.

A WOMAN CAN MAKE OR BREAK HER MAN

I believe that ever since the beginning of time, man's greatest motivating force has been his desire to please his woman. Man's nature has not changed very much. Most men will do anything to attain the women they desire. They will climb mountains, swim rivers, do cartwheels and even work three jobs to impress the women they love. Let's face it. Women have the power to make or break their men.

Most men would probably admit that without women, very little would matter anymore. They are the half that makes men whole. They are the power that has helped men achieve more success than all other forces combined. Of course, fine cars, beautiful homes, jewelry and great vacations are all motivating forces to some people, but if you were to take every materialistic thing on earth and combine their motivational power, it would pale in comparison to the motivational power of women.

THE MIND GOVERNS THE BODY

How do you motivate yourself? That's the real question. We all dance to the beat of a different drummer; one size does not fit all. Not on this dance floor. Each of us has to find the switch that turns on our lights. For some, it's a new car or home. For others, it's the right job or mate. What will make you get dressed, go to school or work, and stay as late as necessary without any complaints?

Finding your sources of inspiration and building on them are essential to your success. Keeping your mind occupied with positive emotions and beautiful, uplifting thoughts can be key.

Self-mastery is the hardest job you will ever undertake. That statement is such a powerful eye-opener that you need to read it again. You can either master yourself or be mastered by the self.

THE MAKING OF A GENIUS

There is a long list of great men who have been labeled as geniuses. If you took the time to study the lives and times of these geniuses, you might make a rather inspirational discovery. The only real difference between ordinary men and geniuses is that geniuses refuse to remain ordinary. They summon the courage from deep inside to fight the hardest battle of all: the battle within themselves. They know that this is a battle that must be won, because they understand the importance of first mastering themselves before attempting to master anything else. Then, whatever follows, whether it's leading a nation, writing poetry or even learning to dance, their victory cannot be denied. Why? Because the very first thing they did was the hardest thing any man will ever do: master himself.

This is easier said than done. It will help if you keep this in mind: the mind is a creature of habit that thrives upon the dominating thoughts it's fed.

You have total control of your thoughts, and that divine privilege makes you master of your fate. With the proper willpower, you can discourage the presence of any thought or emotion while encouraging the presence of another. Your will and self-control are the supreme rulers of your mind. You are supposed to control your mind, not the other way around. Mind control comes from persistence and habit. Of course, it takes concentration of effort. That's why you were given a free will.

Having a free will and total control of your thoughts gives you freedom of choice. You can take control and become one of the strong, or cast yourself upon the rough seas of chance by failing to take control, thus becoming one of the weak. Just remember this, "Only the strong survive."

It's been over forty years since my mother passed away, and not a single day goes by when I don't have cause to stand up and say, "Thank you, mother." I am the man I am today because of her. To me, everyday should be Mother's Day. My mom may have worded it differently when she first said, "Every adversity, every sorrow, every heartache brings with it the possibility of a much greater reward. If you are ready to battle and seek in faith-with an open mind, you'll find that buried in the bitter dust of disappointment there is always an open door to a new horizon." And, she is right.

From the day my mother learned of my learning deficiency, she began planting that thought in the fertile soil of my young mind. She never stopped reminding me I was special, different, and artistic, not autistic. She set out on a mission to make certain I enjoyed a normal childhood and grew up to be a successful young man. She bombarded me every waking moment with love, lessons, teachings, and always positive yes-I-can thoughts. Day after day, she had me repeat so many different positive thinking lines that I began to feel like an encyclopedia. At first, I didn't fully understand half of what she kept repeating to me. I learned whatever she wanted me to learn because I believed in her and instinctively knew it was for my own good.

As I got a little older and read more, I had a better understanding of my learning disability. I also understood quite clearly and believed with great conviction the thoughts my mom was planting in my brain.

By age eleven, I was beginning to believe with God and *The Guide* that I could accomplish anything. I never saw myself as being handicapped and felt pity for the friends and family members who believed I was. "As a man thinketh so he becomes". All praises to the Almighty.

I find the simplicity of the concept to be astounding. (Because the moral to my life story is . . .) the lessons I've learned all along the way is faith can really move mountains. If you truly believe you can succeed, you can . . . if you are ready.

If I had three wishes, one of them would be to make *The Guide* tangible and to ration it out like food stamps. Then I am certain a much larger percentage of this country would become successful. With God and *The Guide*, success is virtually assured.

I couldn't find a way to put the essence of *The Guide* into bottles or cans, but I've placed it within the grasp of my readers right here in this book.

Over the years, I've learned that whether you are in or out of school, the public library is one of the best places to invest your time. The vast amount of information available at every library is mind-boggling. Whatever you're interested in learning, studying, researching, or becoming can be found in the library. Regardless of the subject, your public library has the information you will need.

Should you be seeking financial aid to open any kind of business, you might want to consider applying for a grant. Again, the library has the books that can teach you how and guide you where to apply. If you wanted to return to college or any type of school or research a project, you can apply for a grant to help you accomplish your mission.

Should you ever consider forming a corporation, there is a book you should read. It's called, *Inc and Grow Rich* by C. W. Allen.

There is a book that will help you tremendously on your voyage to your financial independence called *Rich Dad Poor Dad*, by Robert T. Kiyosaki. Get it as soon as you can. Make this a priority. I think you can learn as much from that book in two readings as you will in one year of college. Please get ahold of *Rich Dad Poor Dad*. It teaches financial literacy. It is enlightening, liberating and empowering. Soak up the lessons in it, and then loan it to your children.

IMAGINATION

Albert Einstein once said, "Imagination is more important than education." So let's not end this book without touching briefly on this important subject.

Very few of us are fully aware of the awesome power of our imaginations. Most of us are somewhat aware of its existence and use it occasionally, usually on a very elementary level. Few of us take the time to investigate, study, or exercise it often enough.

There are two parts to the imagination. The first is called the Synthetic Imagination. This part creates nothing. It merely works with what it's fed, like experience and observation.

The second part of the imagination is known as the Creative Imagination. This second part does everything. It is through this faculty that man is able to receive telepathy, inspiration, motivation and all new ideas to create anything he desires. Hence the reasons for the phrase "get creative". This is the part of the imagination great poets, writers, musicians, painters and other artists use to produce great work. These people work hard at developing their Creative Imaginations.

USE IT OR LOSE IT

As surely as any muscle develops through frequent use, so does the Creative Imagination. Center your attention on the task at hand daily, in a quiet and receptive environment, with concentration and effort, willing yourself to produce and believing you can. If you do this as often as you choose, it will be an excellent way to begin to develop your Creative Imagination.

Perhaps there is some truth to the saying that some people are born with it. Who really knows? What is known, and what is important, is the fact it can be cultivated. It can be developed.

Your public library can help with books on this subject. At the library, you can learn much more about imagination, one of nine parts of the human mind. It is a most intricate piece of machinery.

You don't have to be an artist to develop your Creative Imagination. Anyone who desires to be successful, no matter the undertaking, needs to learn to think outside the box.

You can set yourself apart from the crowd, call your own shots and eventually name your own price when you become very good at using your imagination.

In parting, may I remind you that you have absolute control over your thoughts. This divine prerogative gives you control of your earthly destiny. It is your responsibility to use your powers for the attainment of your success.

You are faced with life-changing decisions and choices every hour of every day. You can choose to protect your mind by keeping it busy with a definite plan and purpose and positive emotions, or you can leave it open to bad influences and negative emotions. You were given a will, so use it.

Previously, you may have had a good excuse for not achieving your objectives, but not anymore. You've just been given a road-map to the gates of success. If you neglect to take the trip or stop before you get there, you'll have no one else to blame but yourself.

TO YOU, I OPEN THE GATES OF HOPE

I wrote this book in the hope that it would inspire and improve the lives of everyone who read it, especially my own children and grandchildren. I want them to be proud of my accomplishments in life. More importantly, I want them to be aware of the obstacles I overcame and the courage, pride, and dignity with which I have maintained the struggle against overwhelming odds.

I hope this book serves as the inspirational alarm clock that awakens the genius within you. Reading this book is a big step in the right direction. You must now put what you learned into action.

> Only our actions are noted
> Not what we've read
> And then later quoted

I wish you good health. I wish you success and much happiness, but most importantly, I wish you love.

Conrad Bastien